The Sautar

In Search of Identity and Livelihood

DR. BIRENDRA PRASAD

PRABHAT
PRAKASHAN

Published by
PRABHAT PRAKASHAN
4/19 Asaf Ali Road,
New Delhi-110002 (INDIA)
e-mail: prabhatbooks@gmail.com

ISBN 978-93-5521-756-1
THE SAUTAR: IN SEARCH OF IDENTITY AND LIVELIHOOD
by DR. BIRENDRA PRASAD (IAS)

Edition
First, 2023

Price
₹ 300 (Rupees Three Hundred Only)

Printed at
Japan Art, Delhi

Dedicated to

Parents & Wife,
the inception without whom
my pen would run dry
and I would be nothing.

Author's Note

During my administrative service as the SDM, Kishanganj, District Magistrate of Katihar, Madhepura and Bhagalpur, I had the opportunity to visit the tribal areas. In the course of my work, I interacted with various tribes of the districts namely Munda, Oraon, Malpaharia and Sautar. In North Bihar, the Santhal are known as 'Sautar', in Jharkhand they are called, Santhal and 'Agragri' and 'Shaotal' in Bengal. In Bihar, Sautar is one of the major communities and they form a majority of the state's tribal population. Interested by their way of living, customs and culture, I was drawn to study their social and cultural issues closely.

Sautar - Shautal - Sautar are indigenous tribe residing mainly in West Bengal, Bihar, Jharkhand and Assam. There is also a significant Santhal minority in Nepal, Bhutan and Bangladesh. The Santhal is one of the largest tribal groups in India.

Sautars belong to the Proto-Australoid racial group and are great fighters excelling in archery. The seven groups, who occupy territory farther north, include the Sautar (of India and Nepal), the Bhumij, the Koda, the Mahli, the Ho, and the Agariya. The two remaining groups, the Juango and the Gadaba, are located in the southern portion of India, nearer to the coast of the Bay of Bengal. The Sautar mostly speak Sautari, a member of the Munda language family. In Bihar, the Sautars are mostly landless. Though, some people from the tribe engage themselves in agriculture. The Sautars, both men and women, are masters in archery. They are often considered as martial community by masses. They were hired by the commoners during fights. Two groups of sautars representing the two opponent parties fought each other with arrow. Several sautars were killed due to this practice.

This community has fallen prey to ignorance in the process of socialisation. In independent India, reservations in the field of economic, political and administrative sectors have been made for this tribe. Inspite of all the rules and reservations, they are always ignored and not made a part of the mainstream society and culture.

The ignorance of Sautar community developed gradually when most of their people were converted into Christians. Some also became followers of Chauvinism. Due to this religious conversion, their original beliefs and culture got destroyed. The Aryan groups are the major group which resides in Bihar. The Sautars, on the other hand, are smaller community. This resulted in domination on Sautars by other major Aryan groups. In the cultural structure of India, the cultural indentity and values of Sautars were ignored. The proper polices should be implied for their development. I am trying to present few aspects and facts behind the problems being faced by this community. I hope it will be helpful to the scholars and administrators who are keen to study about Sautar community.

– Dr. Birendra Prasad

Contents

1

The Tribes in Present Bihar

Bihar is as old as civilisation itself and the state reflects a population containing a mixture of various cultures. The different religious groups namely, Hindu, Muslim, Jain, Buddhists, Sikhs and Christians reside in this land of great importance. The population of Bihar also has variations on the basis of race: Aryans, Dravidians and Mongolians. People belonging to diversified linguistic origin such as Bengali, Urdu, Nepali, Marwadi, Gujarati in addition to Bhojpuri, Maithili, Magadhi and Vajjika, have eventually settled in Bihar. Since ancient era it has been the home for extraordinary intellectual work. Associated with 'Samudra Manthan' of Vedic era, Sita of Rama and Karna of Mahabharata, Bihar has a rich cultural background to be proud of. The present society reflects its cultural prosperity adequately.

One of the most attractive features of this ancient state is that it homes thirty unique indigenous groups belonging

Associated with 'Samudra Manthan' of Vedic era, Sita of Rama and Karna of Mahabharata, Bihar has a rich cultural background to be proud of. The present society reflects its cultural prosperity adequately.

to diverse origin. In accordance with The Scheduled Castes and Scheduled Tribes Orders (Amendment) Act, 1976, there are thirty indigenous communities in Bihar and as per the Report of Scheduled Tribes Population Reports of Bihar (2011 Census) there are thirty five tribes divided into different clans namely, Asur, Baiga, Banjara, Bathudi, Bedia, Binjhia, Birhor, Birjia, Chero, Chik Baraik, Gond, Gorait, Ho, Karmali, Kharia, Kharwar, Khond, Kisan, Nagesia, Kora, Korwa, Lohara, Mahli, Mal Paharia, Munda, Oraon, Parhaiya, Sautar, Sauria Paharia, Savar and Kawar Kol Tharu. "Historically, tribal communities were characterized by a lifestyle distinct from agrarian communities. They subsisted on different combinations of shifting cultivation, hunting and gathering of forest products: all activities closely linked with forests. Their cultures celebrated andfostered this close bond with nature while also emphasizing communal ownership and consumption, closely-knit kinship structures, and minimal hierarchies. After Independence, the tribes were accorded special rights and protection under Article 342 of the Constitution with the Government of India's tribal development policy aiming to bring them the benefits of economic development without eroding their traditional culture and identity. Independent India has continued with the 'scheduling' of tribal areas and tribes introduced by the British."

Bihar is an amalgamation of various rich tribal culture and traditions. Almost all tribal villages in the state are inhabited by two or more clans.

In Bihar, the female-male ratio among the tribal population is favourable. This also reflects relatively better status of women in tribal society. Bihar is an amalgamation of various rich tribal culture and traditions. Each of the tribes in Bihar comprises a number of clans. Almost all tribal villages in the state are inhabited by two or more clans. Seldom does one come across a one clan village. Most of the tribes are believed to have migrated from Sub-Himalayan region. Tribal community in Bihar earns their living from agriculture, including shifting cultivation and small cottage industries. Every tribe has their own rituals, dances, festivals and music.

❑

2

Sautar

(Origin, Race, Clan, Population, and Demography)

Sautars are the major tribe of Bihar, hailing from the Austro-Asiatic family. The Austro-Asiatic family is considered to be oldest of all families in South Asia and has considerable existence in South East Asia. The origin and expansion of the Austro-Asiatic populations have been a contentious issue and so far there has been no formidable archaeological or linguistic evidence in favour of any of the hypotheses suggested. Though, in recent times there has been detailed study of genetic studies, elaborating the migration and history of the Austro-Asiatic tribes. The Austro-Asiatic Family in India is representedby the Sautars (now known as Sautar).

When we look back to the long history of ancient India, we come across various other names by which Sautars were called. As our myth narrates, the Aryans followed and occupied the lands and civilization of the original residents. The Aryans called them Ashurs. In Ramayan and Mahabharat they were addressed as Naushad although, they called themselves Kherwars. The name Sautar, was a corruption of Saontar which was adopted by Sautars when they lived in the area around Saont now identified with Silda Pargana in Midnapore district of West Bengal (Skrefsrud, 1868). Sautar is an abbreviation of Samantawala. Samanta was another name given to the country around Saont (W.B Oldham). Sautar is an English form adopted from Hindi which corresponds with the form Saontar used by Bengali speaking people of Bengal (O'Malley,1910; 99). Sir John Shore made the earliest mention of Sautars ever recorded and designated them as Saontars and McPherson pronounced them as Saungtars. Despite this variety of names, most anthropologists agree that Sautar is a name given to this tribe by non-Sautars. In fact Sautars among themselves use the term HOR meaning man (human). Some, living in Bengal and Orissa use term Manjhi to designate their identity (Tribal Religion by J. Troise).

Sautar is an abbreviation of Samantawala. Sautar is an English form adopted from Hindi which corresponds with the form Saontar used by Bengali speaking people of Bengal

The Europeans began documenting about Sautar's origin, customs and traditions during mid-eighteenth century in Chotanagpur plateau in the districts of Hazaribagh, Palamau

On the other hand Colonel Dalton believed that the Sautars came from North-East India, and found their way to the Chotanagpur plateau and the adjoining highlands by the line of their sacred stream, the Damodar River.

and Singhbhum and in the neighbourhood of Midnapore and Birbhum districts. Gradually, the Indian scholars, authors and historian began writing about the Sautars and researching about their origin, tradition and lifestyle.

"On the basis of traditions several theories have been put forward to account for the origin of Sautars. The Rev. L.O. Skrefsrud has conjectured that they lived successively in Persia, Afghanistan and Chinese Tartary, and entered India from the north-west, that they settled in the Punjab and made their way thence to Chotanagpur plateau." (Introduction to Grammar of Sautari Language, 1873).

On the other hand Colonel Dalton believed that the Sautars came from North-East India, and found their way to the Chotanagpur plateau and the adjoining highlands by the line of their sacred stream, the Damodar River. In support of this theory he cited certain remarkable coincidences of custom and language between the Sautars and some of the aboriginal tribes on the north-eastern frontiers of India, from which he inferred a connection in the remote past. This theory of a north-eastern origin was also accepted by Sir William Hunter in the Annals of Rural Bengal.

Colonel Waddell, again, regards the Sautar tradition of their wanderings “as a record of actual tribal progress from the central alluvial valley of the Ganges south-westward to the hills, under pressure of the Aryan invasion of the valley from the north”.

“The theory which seems to me capable of proof is that Sautars, or rather the people of whom they are a portion, occupied the country on both sides of the Ganges, but more especially that in the north. Starting from the north-east, they gradually worked their way up the valley of the Ganges till we find them in the neighborhood of Benares, with their headquarters near Mirzapur. Here the main body which had kept the northern bank of the river, crossed and heading southwards, came to the Vindhya hills. This obstruction deflected them to the left, and they at length found themselves on the tableland of Chotanagpur”. Dr. Campbell further believed that the traditions point to a remote past and not to the recent migration inside the Chotanagpur plateau.

“The theory which seems to me capable of proof is that Sautars, or rather the people of whom they are a portion, occupied the country on both sides of the Ganges, but more especially that in the north.

“Efforts have been made to identify the countries, rivers, forts, etc. mentioned in the traditions of the Sautars with those of similar names in Chotanagpur. Localities have in many instances been found bearing traditional names, and the inference has been drawn that it was here that the traditions of the Sautars took their rise, and that their institutions were formed. But only a slight knowledge of these traditions is necessary to show that they belong to a much more remote period than the location of the Sautars in Chotanagpur, and to countries separated from it by many hundreds of miles".(A. Campbell, Traditional Migration of the Sautar Tribe, Indian Antiquary, 1894, pp. 103-4.).

"A people whose only means of recording facts consists of tying knots in strings, and who have no bards to hand down a national epic by oral tradition, can hardly be expected to preserve the memory of their past long enough or accurately enough for their accounts of it to possess any historical value. If, however, the legends of the Sautars are regarded as an account of recent migrations, their general purport will be found to be fairly in accord with actual facts." (Sir Herbert Risley).

The earliest settlements which Sautar tradition speaks of, those in Hihiri Pipiri and Chai Champa lie on the north-western frontier of the tableland of Hazaribagh and in the direct line of advance of the numerous Hindu immigrants from Bihar.

"If the date of the taking of this fort by Ibrahim Ali were assumed to be about 1340 A.D, the subsequent migrations of which the tribal legends speak would fill up the time intervening between the departure of the Sautars from Chai Champa and their settlement in the present Sautar Parganas. Speaking generally, these recent migrations have been to the east, which is the direction they might prima facie have been expected to follow. The earliest settlements which Sautar tradition speaks of, those in Hihiri Pipiri and Chai Champa lie on the north-western frontier of the tableland of Hazaribagh and in the direct line of advance of the numerous Hindu immigrants from Bihar. The influx of Hindus has in fact driven the Sautars eastward is beyond doubt, and the line which they are known to have followed in their retreat corresponds on the whole with that attributed to them in their tribal legends." (Tribes and Castes of Bengal. Vol. 11, pp. 225-6).

Belonging to the Proto-Australoid racial group, the Sautar (Sautars) linguistically belong to the Mundari group of Austro-Asiatic linguistic family. The ethnological study of Indian subcontinent discloses six main races of people involved in different cultures and tradition. The earliest traced races Negritos, Proto-Australoids or Austrics, Mongoloid, Mediter raneanor Dravidians, Western Brachycephals and Nordics (related to Aryan race). Among these divisions, the Munda, Ho and Sautars belong to the Austric group of indigenous peoples.

"The Austric tribes are said to 'form the bedrock of the people' and were the main builders of the Indus Valley Civilization. They cultivated rice and vegetables and made sugar from sugarcane. Their language has survived in the Kol or Munda (Mundari), Ho and Sautars (Sautari)" (culturopedia.com/tribes/the races of INDIA and Dr. B.S. Guha).

The Sautars can be identified by their distinctive physical structure. The Proto-Australoids, the race Sautars belong to, were ancient hunter-gatherer people who descended from the first major wave of anatomically modern humans to leave Africa around 50,000 years ago. They are characterised by gracile body types, they are thought to have had dark skin colour, approaching black, and wavy or curly black hair, low forehead, thick lips and wide jaw.

Histories of Sautars can also be traced from songs and folklore of Sautar tribe. Historians from different region have come and wrote different things regarding them and large populations believe that is only the truth about Sautars. Pandit Raghunath Murmu, who develops Sautari manuscript, written Sautars are from Pre-Aryan period and they were the real great fighters during British regime. Sautars were the first who fought against Permanent Settlement Act of Lord Cornwallis during 1855. It was during late 1850, when Sidhu Murmu, Kanhu Murmu, Chand Murmu and Bhairo Murmu hoarded around 85,000 Sautars to wage a war against British to object all the law which were objectionable to them at that point of time.

The sautars (Sautars) have 12 clans and each have further sub divisions. The patrilineal subdivisions are based on descent. There prevails a Sautari myth base on which the divisions are made. According to their belief, Pilchu Haram and Pilchu Burhi gave birth to seven sons and seven daughters. The sons and daughters married among themselves and formed seven exogamous clans. With time, five more clans were formed, summing upto be total twelve clans.

Murmu, Hansda, Mardi, Soren, Hembram, Tudu, Kisku, Baskey, Besra, Chonde, Gondwar and Panwariya are the twelve divisions on the basis of clans. They are further subdivided in many sub-clans. Following are the sub clans headed by the main Sautar clan:

The sautars (Sautars) have 12 clans and each have further sub divisions. The patrilineal subdivisions are based on descent. There prevails a Sautari myth base on which the divisions are made.

Katihar has the largest Sautar population (79,899). More than three fourth tribal population of Katihar, Banka, Jamui, Kishanganj, Araria and Madhepura are Sautars, followed by Saharsa which constitutes 72 percent of Sautar population and Purnia homes 65 percent. The sex ratio of the Sautars is above 900 in Bihar and its child sex ratio is higher than the national average ratio.

Sex Ratio

(Source: Office of the Registrar General, India BIHAR DATA HIGHLIGHTS: THE SCHEDULED TRIBES Census of India 2001 & 2011)

Age groups	2001			2011		
	All STs (India)	All STs (Bihar)	Sautars	All STs (India)	All STs (Bihar)	Sautars
All ages	978	929	950	990	958	966
0-6 yrs.	972	975	976	957	969	971

The Work Participation Rate (WPR) of the ST population of Bihar is 45.2 percent which is lower than that of all STs at the national level (49.1 per cent). The Sautars having recorded 48.5 percent WPR is close to the national average.

Language

The Sautari language can be broadly classified into two categories, Dravidian and Munda or Austric. The Sautars mostly belong to the Austro-Asiatic language family. In 1920s, Pandit Raghunath Murmu developed manuscript of the Sautars which was called "Ol Chiki". Initially, "Ol Chiki" was not appreciated and regarded as a mimeograph. Also, it was considered to not have any characteristics that a language should possess. Later, scholars and researchers studied and it was found that Ol Chiki is alphabetic. The syllabic properties of other Indian scripts like Devanagari are not contained in Ol Chiki.

The Sautari language has close similarity with the Bengali language and it is also believed that the language of the Sautars is literally an older version of Indo-Aryan languages. Hindi is widely spoken and written by the Sautars of Bihar.

Generated from Gahla Tudag, Ol Chiki uses 30 letters inclusive of five basic diacritics, six basic vowels and three additional vowels. Until nineteenth century, the Sautars do not have any written script. Being a recent development, it was necessary for the Sautars to possess a unique script of its own which did not amalgamate any feature of both Indic and Roman scripts. In the year 1925, Pandit

Raghunath Murmu revised and created the modern Ol Chiki script. A gamut of subjects where covered n the 450 books that Pandit Murmu authored. Darege Dhan, Sidhu-Kanhu, Bidu Chandan and Kherwal Bir are some of the applauded works of his. Pandit Raghunath Murmu is popular as Guru Gomke among all the Sautars and the title was bestowed to him by the Mayurbhanj Adibasi Mahasabh.

The need for the Sautars to be educated in their own language was felt by Pandit Raghunath Murmu but initially, non-existence of text books and properly trained teachers to impart knowledge made it hard to materialize.

The need for the Sautars to be educated in their own language was felt by Pandit Raghunath Murmu but initially, non-existence of text books and properly trained teachers to impart knowledge made it hard to materialize. There was also the absence of a sizeable body of literature in the language in printed form and the lack of a general will and determination among the literate Sautar masses to learn the script and to use it. Pandit Murmu then realize that that the Ol Chiki should equip itself properly before claiming to be a part of education system. But, In Bihar, most of the Sautars wanted to retain the Roman script.

According to Dr. B.B. Hembrom, "The Sautari language has its own original existence, its own entity. Bengali language cannot be written in English script and vice-versa. If anybody ventures to write the Sautari Language in English or Bengali script or Hindi or Oriya script, he is just going to put a garland on the neck of a red hot statue, and if it happens so accidentally and unfortunately, within a short period the Sautari language will be phonetically deformed. Consequently it will lose its glamour, its original beauty, and in the long run this resourceful language will be compelled to live a crippled life among the healthy language of the other peoples of India. The great diversity of Sautari language due to regional impact resulted in the confusion and disintegration among its members, sometime earlier which are in the process of being re-organised with the help of a new linguistic movement."

Sautari has now made its way of becoming an optional subject for matriculation in Jharkhand, Bihar and West Bengal. 12 dictionaries like works have been published in Sautari language.

Sautari has now made its way of becoming an optional subject for matriculation in Jharkhand, Bihar and West Bengal. 12 dictionaries like works have been published in Sautari language. Sautari to English and English to Sautari dictionaries have also been published.

The Sautari language and literature has already been recognised by the Central Government and State Government of Bihar, Jharkhand, West Bengal and Orissa in:

Sautar (Origin, Race, Clan, Population, and Demography)

1. Bihar Secondary School Examination Board, Patna and Jharkhand Secondary School Examination Board, Jharkhand have accepted Sautari Language/Literature as optional paper in Matriculation level.
2. The Govt. of Bihar is first to publish a journal named "Hor Sambad" since 1947 which is now continue by Govt. of Jharkhand and Govt. of West Bengal Publishing Sautari magazine "Puchhim Bangla" regularly and recognise Ol chiki script for Sautari in 1979.
3. The state Govt. of Jharkhand, Bihar, West Bengal and Orissa have already initiated action plans for imparting education in mother tongue for the Sautar students in primary schools.
4. The University Grants Commission, Delhi has started imparting education and conferring Post-Graduate Degree in Sautari language and literature.
5. The Bihar Public Service Commission offers Sautari Language/Literature as optional paper for its competitive Examination.
6. The Govt. of Bihar has been conducting Sautari Examination for its officers posted in Sautari speaking areas in Bihar for administrative purposes/reason.
7. Vishwa Bharti University, Santiniketan has been imparting education in Sautari language for the last 24 years or so.

The Universities of Jharkhand and Bihar, namely Ranchi University, Ranchi, Vinoba Bhave University, Hazaribagh, Sidu Kanhu University Dumka, and Baba Tilka Majhi University, Bhagalpur are conducting examinations of Sautari language/literature in the Post-Graduate level.

❑

Report of Scheduled Tribes' Caste wise Population Reports of Bihar according to 2011.

S.No.	Districts	Asur, Agaria	Baiga	Banjara	Bathudi	Bedia	Binjhia	Birhor	Birjia	Chero	Chik Baraik	Gond	Gorait	Ho	Karmali	Kharia, Dhelki Kharia, Dudh Kharia, Hill Kharia	Kharwar	Khond	Kisan, Nage-sia	Kora, Mudi-kora	Korwa	Lohara, Lohra	Mahli	Mal Paharia, Kumar-bhag Paharia	Mun-da, Patar	Oraon, Dhangar (Oraon)	Par-haiya	Santal	Sauria Pah-aria	Savar	Kawar	Kol	Tharu	TOTAL
1	2	3	4	5	6	7	8	9	10	11	12	13	14	15	16	17	18	19	20	21	22	23	24	25	26	27	28	29	30	31	32	33	34	35
1	PATNA	40	11	120	0	27	3	47	0	14	36	1830	13	100	36	246	456	23	39	25	19	193	79	14	503	1961	0	1166	9	0	51	339	117	7517
2	NALANDA	30	4	108	0	1	0	0	2	7	4	3	0	0	0	647	9	0	1	22	0	16	6	4	53	140	0	114	28	0	22	13	2	1236
3	ROHTAS	72	19	28	1	0	2	0	2	4927	328	3387	5	23	0	389	6917	1	12	4	68	121	19	0	268	11059	6	78	15	0	48	1388	1	29188
4	BHABHUA	1878	62	1	,0	0	13	0	0	3600	56	14813	241	9	17	778	29045	12	0	268	247	111	0	0	54	4790	0	25	0	0	109	3	0	56132
5	BHOJPUR	25	8	12	0	0	0	1	0	93	1	10344		14	49	60	934	0	0	6	0	108	14	3	58	195	0	47	0	0	5	160	7	12144
6	BUXAR	41	10	39	0	0	0	0	0	9	15	20974	39	3	61	287	4323	1	0	4	2	84	4	0	18	80	0	53	3	0	24	22	0	26096
7	GAYA	31	11	4	0	0	0	6	0	7	8	40	0	89	0	181	289	3	14	2	0	155	20	7	291	208	182	97	119	0	1	234	22	2021
8	JEHANABAD	8	1	23	0	2	0	0	1	29	0	4	65	1	1	304	6	0	0	471	0	36	8	0	40	74	3	134	5	0	0	22	1	1239
9	ARWAL	0	2	39	0	0	0	0	41	5	3	1	0	0	0	164	4	0	43	141	1	3	6	1	11	96	0	0	0	0	0	2	2	565
10	NAWADAH	145	14	1	0	0	0	81	10	11	8	9	0	0	7	176	18	0	0	17	0	3	20	10	34	94	0	566	30	1	2	8	2	1267
11	AURANG-ABAD	29	27	56	0	0	0	0	0	5	0	66	25	0	0	30	153	0	0	1	3	25	7	5	10	313	2	6	0	0	0	29	6	798
12	SARAN	49	11	1	0	0	4	5	0	206	169	33191	3	2	2	233	458	0	2	1	0	195	28	1	43	133	0	128	0	0	10	33	0	34908
13	SIWAN	75	32	7	0	0	0	2	7	189	182	75537	29	29	0	540	5544	0	1	1	0	123	19	0	17	397	0	24	2	0	7	45	3	82812
14	GOPALGANJ	32	31	6	0	0	0	7	25	19	28	51425	383	70	0	805	4471	5	2	72	0	170	47	3	12	397	24	16	0	0	12	18	1	58081
15	MUZAFFAR-PUR	117	29	68	5	82	0	2	0	252	3	1114	1	14	0	286	1995	0	1	6	0	136	7	1	47	192	0	33	3	0	29	98	28	4549
16	SITAMARHI	20	6	43	0	1104	0	0	0	2	0	243	0	23	0	47	8	0	0	2	0	51	17	1	12	1005	0	15	1	0	54	223	22	2899
17	SHEOHAR	3	9	0	0		0	0	0	0	0	2	0	0	0	124	0	0	0	36	0	38	13	0	0	6	0	7	0	0	0	3	0	241
18	W. CHAM-PARAN	124	32	43	0		1	8	0	2944	144	31102	10	19	137	4699	0	0	0	20	0	882	20	101	1947	40951	1	135	304	4	57	67	159040	242792

19	E. CHAM-PARAN	85	17	6	0	0	1	2	0	140	1	9278	11	1	0	173	580	0	1	10	0	121	6	1	37	861	0	25	0	0	5	99	5	11466
20	VAISHALI	19	4	60	0	0	0	0	0	0	11	295	0	9	0	172	488	11	0	9	0	91	5	75	92	197	1	11	0	0	23	401	6	1980
21	DARBHANGA	109	12	148	3	0	0	0	0	41	277	42	0	6	0	742	99	4	2	16	24	3	36	0	63	523	0	315	15	9	9	40	5	2543
22	MADHUBANI	391	19	3	0	0	0	5	1	44	108	37	0	1	778	0	8	10	1	1	0	18	12	59	75	175	1	1317	21	2	1	26	409	3523
23	SAMASTI-PUR	3	1	75	0	0	0	0	0	5	0	196	0	22	0	203	205	14	0	5	0	49	61	1	206	190	1	110	1	0	80	352	9	1789
24	SAHARSA	17	4	0	0	0	0	0	0	5	0	33	0	0	0	141	41	0	0	128	0	0	5	0	38	71	0	4157	2	40	4	35	0	4721
25	SUPAUL	85	3	649	2	9	0	0	0	20	3	23	0	1	0	402	16	0	0	39	22	16	31	45	21	4441	6	2655	314	0	0	2	0	8805
26	MADHEPURA	76	3	20	0	0	0	0	0	32	10	7	2	0	0	450	1	3	0	99	1	65	0	930	107	454	0	8279	132	1	3	0	0	10675
27	PURNEA	108	12	0	1	0	2	2	0	0	18	248	0	37	8	42	968	0	9719	99	0	824	998	736	1564	30154	0	76708	23	4	54	246	1	122576
28	ARARIA	86	25	6	6	0	1	2	0	39	15	36	0	2	1	583	52	0	156	97	0	385	397	8	712	3850	0	25473	62	0	1	90	221	32306
29	KISHAN-GANJ	40	3	19	0	215	1	6	47	37	5	167	0	43	0	142	40	5	2	15	5	179	107	174	1645	3735	0	45390	1	2	5	1	7	52038
30	KATIHAR	76	17	1101	0	26	7	0	2	21	664	664	1	79	28	513	22383	30	18930	629	14	2949	659	14	5711	30823	408	79899	442	7	77	90	5	166269
31	BHAGALPUR	14	1	2	0	299	0	191	55	0	0	1121	6	34	0	77	40661	10	0	8	9	93	46	0	84	6277	0	14743	345	4	35	178	4	64297
32	BANKA	65	2	3	0	0	0	1	1	0	2	129	3	0	0	10	19	0	0	811	1	45	531	0	11	28	5	70164	4	2	0	4271	2	76110
33	MUNGER	37	67	19	0	0	0	0	0	1	5	258	2	44	0	474	112	1	5	4097	18	0	6	29	87	233	6	13208	48	0	0	985	3	19745
34	LAKHISARAI	4	16	5	0	0	0	1	2	0	0	12	0	1	29	320	7	0	0	5594	5	21	7	0	26	18	0	332	1	0	130	7	2	6540
35	SHEIKH-PURA	3	1	0	0	0	0	0	0	13	25	1	0	9	0	333	7	0	0	121	0	0	1	0	9	37	0	18	1	0	0	0	0	579
36	JAMUI	145	13	1	0	1	0	0	0	21	6	7	0	9	40	357	846	1	0	3666	6	377	640	1	61	113	1	60367	1	4	2	1135	1	67822
37	KHAGARIA	24	2	0	0	0	7	0	0	3	0	3	0	0	0	197	35	0	0	29	0	1	9	0	18	26	0	135	0	0	5	7	2	503
38	BEGUSARAI	23	2	0	0	5	0	1	0	0	0	96		18	0	26	207	0	0	8	6	31	41	1	43	175	0	126	0	0	6	60	3	878
	TOTAL	4129	543	2716	18	1771	42	370	196	12741	2135	256738	839	712	1194	15353	121405	134	28931	16580	451	7718	3932	2225	14028	144472	647	406076	1932	80	871	10732	159939	1219650

SANTHAL(BIHAR) CENSUS 2011

S.No.	Districts	Santhal
1	**2**	**3**
1	KATIHAR	79899
2	PURNEA	76708
3	BANKA	70164
4	JAMUI	60367
5	KISHANGANJ	45390
6	ARARIA	25473
7	BHAGALPUR	14743
8	MUNGER	13208
9	MADHEPURA	8279
10	SAHARSA	4157
11	SUPAUL	2655
12	MADHUBANI	1317
13	NAWADAH	566
14	LAKHISARAI	332
15	DARBHANGA	315
16	W. CHAMPARAN	135
17	KHAGARIA	135
18	JEHANABAD	134
19	SARAN	128
20	BEGUSARAI	126
21	SAMASTIPUR	110
22	GAYA	97
23	ROHTAS	78
24	BUXAR	53
25	BHOJPUR	47
26	MUZAFFARPUR	33
27	BHABHUA	25
28	E. CHAMPARAN	25
29	SIWAN	24
30	SHEIKHPURA	18
31	GOPALGANJ	16
32	SITAMARHI	15
33	VAISHALI	11
34	SHEOHAR	7
35	AURANGABAD	6
36	ARWAL	0
	TOTAL	**404796**

ST Bihar (Census 2011)

S.No.	Caste	Male	Female	Total	% of Total
1	2	3	4	5	6
1	Santal	2,06,506	1,99,570	4,06,076	30.38
2	Gond	1,29,927	1,26,811	2,56,738	19.21
3	Tharu	81,236	78,703	1,59,939	11.97
4	Oraon, Dhangar (Oraon)	73,917	70,555	1,44,472	10.81
5	Kharwar	66,110	59,701	1,25,811	9.41
6	Kisan, Nagesia	14,937	13,994	28,931	2.16
7	Kora, Mudi-kora	8,398	8,182	16,580	1.24
8	Munda, Patar	7,226	6,802	14,028	1.05
9	Chero	6,589	6,152	12,741	0.87
10	Kharia, Dhelki Kharia, Dudh Kharia, Hill Kharia	5,852	5,717	11,569	0.87
11	Kol	5,536	5,199	10,735	0.80
12	Lohara, Lohra	4,033	3,685	7,718	0.58
13	Mahli	2,169	1,963	4,132	0.31
14	Asur, Agaria	2,114	2,015	4,129	0.31
15	Banjara	1,371	1,338	2,709	0.20
16	Mal Paharia, Kumarbhag Paharia	1,155	1,070	2,225	0.17
17	Chik Baraik	1,091	1,044	2,135	0.16
18	Sauria Paharia	974	958	1,932	0.14
19	Bedia	938	839	1,777	0.13
20	Kawar	456	412	868	0.06
21	Gorait	405	431	836	0.06
22	Ho	375	340	715	0.05
23	Parhaiya	325	322	647	0.05
24	Baiga	276	267	543	0.04
25	Korwa	235	217	452	0.03
26	Birhor	187	190	377	0.03
27	Karmali	145	132	277	0.02
28	Birjia	113	95	208	0.02
29	Khond	81	53	134	0.01
30	Savar	44	36	80	0.01
31	Bathudi	12	6	18	0.00
32	Binjhia	6	9	15	0.00
	All Schedule Tribes	**6,82,516**	**6,54,057**	**13,36,573**	100.00

3
Religion and Beliefs

Sautars are the followers of Sari Dharam and Sarna religion. Jaheraera, Marangburu, Manjhi are the Gods which they worship. Marangburu, the God of the mountains is also one of the most important Gods to whom they offer prayers. Animists by nature, they sacrifice animals to their gods. Village deity of Gramdeuta is also worshiped. The priest of Sautars is called Naiki and the shaman Ujha. Pilchuhadam and Budi are their ancestral deities.

The Sautar pantheon includes about 150 spirit deities generally called Bongas. These deities include a large number of separate classes, impossible to enumerate here. Some relate to the sub clan, but even here we must distinguish between the place of origin of the clan and its ancestral spirit. Each village has a sacred grove. They are generally benevolent. The forest bongas, however, are malevolent, and include the souls of people who died an unnatural death.

Hindu influence is particularly notable in the appearance of Hindu goddesses as tutelary deities of Sautar ojhas. On the one hand, these goddesses patronize Sautar witches and introduce disease; on the other hand, their patronage is necessary to combat the same evils. Hindu symbols, such as the trident, have become potent ritual paraphernalia of the Sautar ojha.

Hindu influence is particularly notable in the appearance of Hindu goddesses as tutelary deities of Sautar ojhas.

The village priest (naeke) is identified, with his wife, as representative of the original Sautar couple. Their functions are mainly related to festivals and recurrent annual ceremonies. He consecrates the animals offered to the sacred grove deities. He often compares himself with the Brahman of the encompassing society.

The Sautar ojha, a healer and diviner, has several functions. He drives away the malevolent deities, divines the causes of disease, administers remedies according to considerable medical knowledge, and expels pain from the body. He learns his basic magical formulas (mantras) from his master, but he also adds to them from his own experience. An important element in his repertoire is the sacrifice of his own blood (conceived as menstrual blood) to the bongas, for which he receives a fee. In the rationalization of his practice he employs several Hindu concepts, yet remains fundamentally within the Sautar cultural framework. This position between two Cultures enables him to interpret his own culture and society.

There is a belief prevalent among the Sautars about creation of the world. According to their belief, the primitive world was filled with only water and God had the problem in creating the land, where man can live.

There is a belief prevalent among the Sautars about creation of the world. According to their belief, the primitive world was filled with only water and God had the problem in creating the land, where man can live. When land was not molded yet, amphibians where the first living beings created by God as all amphibian animals can live both on land and water. Hence, seven animals namely, crab, crocodile, alligator, eel, Pawn, earthworm and tortoise were created. But, creation of land was important. So, God invited the kings of all animals to help him and solve this major problem. The kings came one by one and no one had a solution of this problem. Earthworm was the last animal to come and it is believed that it had succeeded in finding ways to create land. The King of earthworm after seven days and seven nights ate the bottom of water and excreted in on the back of tortoise that is swimming at the top.

The tortoise anchored himself on the both side firmly and brought up the earth and thus earth was shaped. That is why there is a belief among Sautars that earthquakes are result of movement of tortoise. In otherwords, whentortoise moves or shakes, earthquakes occur in earth. Sautar myth about the creation of world is substantially different from myth associated with creation of world among the other indigenous peoples of India and in many sense it is unique that it ascribe the creation of earth with the help of amphibian animals, specially the earthworm and tortoise. This is all about the story of creation of earth.

Although, Sautar do not strictly believe that they have descended from animals, however, they assume that there is some connection between animal and human being.

There is another interesting myth about creation of human beings. Again here, this myth is substantially different from the many similar myths that are prevalent among the other peoples. Unlike others, Sautar myth is more associated with nature and animals. Although, Sautar do not strictly believe that they have descended from animals, however, they assume that there is some connection between animal and human being. It reflects many other Sautar beliefs and myth. According to the myth, God created two heavenly birds—Has and Hasil, out of his hair. Then these two birds started flying in the sky. These bird could survive early state of earth, where all earth was covered with water, as they could mediate the opposite elements heaven and earth. It is believed that they flew below the sun and above the earth thus making the contact between the both worlds. After flying several days, they built the nest on the earth and laid the eggs. They are cosmic eggs, out of which two creatures; human male and human female are born—Pilchu Haram and Pilchu Burhi. Both these myths creation of world and mankind refer the birds and animal as ancestors. Thus, Sautar concept of life begins with animals. Therefore, clans' names are after the name of animals.

Totemism

After creation of earth, Pilchu Haram and Pilchu Burhi gave birth to seven sons and seven daughters. In later stage they married among themselves thus forming seven exogamous clans. With the passage of time, five more groups were formed. A total 12 clans is found among the Sautars. They are Hansdak, Murmu, Hembrom, Soren, Kisku, Tudu, Marndi, Baske, Besra, Chonre, Puria and Bedea. An affiliation or sacred contact is believed to link these clans and their respective totems. Therefore, each of the names of clans are derived from either from the plants or animals species. There is a belief that is prevalent among the Sautars that totems have some connection with the deeds or birth of ancestors of the clans. Hansdak clan members claim to be of the highest status as they have derived from the name of their clan from first ancestors. The term has designates wild goose while dak in Sautari means water.

This clan is, therefore, linked to the original state of world and first ancestors. It is the most senior among the all clans of the Sautars, since it is related to myth of creation. Moreover, swan or goose is not just a water animal. It builds nest on earth, walks on earth and flies on sky.

Next in order are the Murmus who are represented by the Nilgai or the antelope. According to the myth of genesis of this clans, it is said that ancestors of this clan hunted first the antelope as animal and in other words, it is this animal which was first sacrificed by Sautars. Since this time, Sautars started hunting and eating of animals and subsequently become fond of hunting and eating of flesh. The antelope being purely a land animal is responsible for the destruction of Sautars among the Sautars as opposed to swan who combines the four elements and stands for humanity and creation of human beings. The Hansdak and the Murmu are the two superior clans of the Sautars. As the story goes, Hansdak are given the status of advisors and the Murmus are the priest.

According to the myth of genesis of this clans, it is said that ancestors of this clan hunted first the antelope as animal and in other words, it is this animal which was first sacrificed by Sautars.

The Kiskus have kingfishers bird as their totem and come third in the hierarchy. They are regarded as kings and are given the Royal status. Hembrom are fourth in order and have betel nut as their totem. It is believed that the ancestor of the Hembrom clan was born with a betel nut

If any of the clan members sees a dead totem, he observes the death rituals. Eating or hunting the totem is prohibited. The reason lies in the nature of the totems and the elements they are connected with.

string around his waist. There are also those who believe that their ancestor was actually born under a betel nut tree, which is totally hard and solid.

Marndis are linked with grass or type of weed and are traders. The Sorens are soldiers or warriors and are linked to the constellation of stars. The Tudus are musicians and have accepted owl as their totem. Baskes are cooks and associated stale rice. They have believed to offered stale rice to the Gods and are thus prohibited from eating it. Bedeas have sheep as their totem and believed to have no personal own much like the animal they revere. They are not found in now days and believed to mix with other clans. Lastly are the Paurias and Chonres who have pigeons and lizard respectively as their totems. It is found that in most of the cases that the only animals the clan members could hunt were made their totem, which perhaps restricted them endangering the species.

So strong are their feelings towards these totemic species that they respect them as their won clan members. If any of the clan members sees a dead totem, he observes the death rituals. Eating or hunting the totem is prohibited. The reason lies in the nature of the totems and the elements they are connected with. In first place the marriage is forbidden between the water and land i.e. swan (Hansdak) and antelope (Murmu). It is restricted between "lower heaven" and "lower earth" i.e. Kingfisher and weed (Kisku and Marndi), also "upper heaven" (Hembrom) and "upper earth"(Soren). Secondly, marriage is prohibited between three heavenly birds (Owl, hawk and pigeon). The totem also defined some relationship between consumed and consumer. The pigeon that is the prey of the hawk along with the lizard eats Rice and the owl also hunts this lizard. Therefore, initially the Chonres did not marry with Besras and Tudus. But presently this restriction is no longer followed and the marriages take place between all clan members.

The names of the sub-clan are derived from plants and animals. Out of the 16 sub-clans that were available in the area, nine trace their origins to certain animals.

Each of these clans is further divided into several sub clans; each one upholds a distinctive myth and set of customs that differentiates it from the others, including kinds of food taken, ornaments, worn and worship of the spirits or Gods (Bongas). Even the sacrifices vary during the rituals vary from one sub-clan to another. The names of the sub-clan are derived from plants and animals. Out of the 16 sub-clans that were available in the area, nine trace their origins to certain animals. For examples, Chilbinda hansdak derived its name from the ancestor who killed an eagle, "Jihu hansdak" from Jihu or babbler bird. Sole-Hemborm does not eat eels as it is believed its ancestor had been saved by it while ferrying flooded river. The kahu-Besras are prohibited to kill crows. The totem exercises powerful influence on the habit of the Sautars.

Sautar souls become bongas three generations after death, provided that the correct rituals have been performed. At cremation, some bones are collected by the main mourner (usually the eldest son) and kept for a while under the rafters of the house.

Death and Afterlife

Sautar souls become bongas three generations after death, provided that the correct rituals have been performed. At cremation, some bones are collected by the main mourner (usually the eldest son) and kept for a while under the rafters of the house. They are washed and fed ritually by female mourners with milk, rice beer, and sacred water. Thus, the mourning ritual displays the central Sautar symbolism of flower and bone. The feeding of bones that are crowned by flowers expresses the complementarities of the principle of descent (bone) and the principle of affinity. The chief mourner is possessed by and impersonates the dead and is questioned by the village priest. This dialogue aims at providing the deceased with the wherewithal of the other world. A year later, the bones are immersed in water, a ritual involving sacrifice of a goat. The dead now becomes an ancestor known by name; one month later the recitation of a ritual text releases him from identity to become a nameless ancestor. He now joins other ancestors in the ancestral room of the house and partakes in the offering of rice beer to the ancestors. Now his shadow, which was roaming between the worlds, goes to Hanapuri, the abode of the dead. Here Jom Raja, king of the dead, rules; the passage from there to the state of becoming a bonga is never made explicit.

The land of the dead is conceptualized as a place where certain individuals acquire the source of magic powers, while others are simply rewarded according to the way they have acted during their life.

The land of the dead is conceptualized as a place where certain individuals acquire the source of magic powers, while others are simply rewarded according to the way they have acted during their life. While the yogi returns to the world and achieves immortality, simple men endure the justice of Jom Raja. The idea of afterlife has both Hindu and Christian influence.

❑

4

The Society and Customs

(Marriage and Customary Laws)

Sautar Marriage

Marriage signifies prosperity and inception of new life of the Sautar community. In spite of some social turbulence in social norms during the past century in Sautar communities, the institution of marriage is very strong. In Sautari language, marriage is called 'Bapla'. A secure environment is needed for every society to commemorate its species, so does Sautars. Many believe that Sautar marriage is more of a private affair than a public one. They follow the tradition of expressing love to each other, introverted. Yet, for centuries, the Sautar marriages have been publicly celebrated following all the ceremonial and ritualistic rules. Tradition, culture, religion and Sautar marriage rules are perfectly reflected throughthe ceremony. Along with

In Sautari language, marriage is called 'Bapla'. A secure environment is needed for every society to commemorate its species, so does Sautars.

the rules and customs, singing, dancing, playing of musical instruments, feast and merrymaking are important parts of a Sautar marriage ceremony.

The decision of marriage of a boy and girl of Sautar community is made by either their family members or by themselves. The usual form of marriage is monogamy. Though, bigamy is also allowed. Levirate and Surrogate marriage are possible depending on the situation. Pre-marital relation within lineage group is not allowed. But in case of other lineage group it is excused and finally results in marriage or social segregation. Marriage may take place between boys and girls of two lineages but generally it is avoided. They generally follow village exogamy. Usual way of acquiring bride is by bride-price (Gonog) and through the consent of parents of boys and girls. But marriage by exchange, elopement service and love may also take place followed by customs only. A woman made pregnant by another male can be socially accepted and converted in marriage. Divorce can be obtained easily; however, some alimony has to be given whole divorcee. If marriages are undertaken within one's own group, such couples are ostracized and chased away from society. There is also the practice of the son-in-law staying in his in-laws' house.

When revising the history of Sautar marriage, we come across two mythological names, Pilchu hadam and Pilchu bhudi. Folklore is believed that, Sautar's world started with them and they were the first couple to get married. Rest followed and modified in due course of time. According to the documentations made by scholars and anthropologists, Sautar culture has diverse versions and ways. Edward Westermarck defined Sautar's marriage as "a more or less durable connection between male and female, lasting beyond the mere act of propagation till after the birth of the offspring." The anthropological handbook Notes and Queries (1951) defined marriage as "a union of a man and a woman such that children of the woman are recognized as legitimate by both parents".

Sautar marriages are divided into many catergories and are exogamous innature. 'Bapla' are of twelve types namely Sanga Bapla, Kadam Bapla, Kirin Bapla, Upagir Bapla, Tunki Dipil Bapla, Itut Bapla, Nirbelok Bapla, Diku Bapla, Sange Bariyat, Haram Bariiyat, Gardi-Jawain.

The marriage ceremony takes five days and involves various, often complex, rituals. Madwa is the centre of the courtyard where some of the marriage rituals take place. A branch of the Mahua, blackberry, mango or Sal tree is planted in the courtyard. Sautars believe that benevolent spirits dwell in these trees. On either side of the branch, two earthen pots are placed and these pots are filled with water. Two unmarried girls of the village have the responsibility to carry along the earthen pots. These pots are a symbol meant to remind the bride of her friendship with the village people.

Sautars regard marriage as pure and sacred. All customs are strictly followed during marriage to maintain its serenity. First few steps are common in every type of marriages. Parents of boys or girls will appoint an interlocutor called Raibaar. Raibaar is the one who, mediate in initiating talk about marriage proposal to either family. Generally Raibaar is known by both the family, and have jesting relation with both boy, girl and parents too.

Sautars regard marriage as pure and sacred. All customs are strictly followed during marriage to maintain its serenity.

Gidi-chumara (Marriage Reception) is the day when the senior women of the village arrive to bless the bride and groom with grass and grains of rice which are kept in a basket. Akhur, the high wooden turmeric crusher is used to make turmeric powder. It is then soaked in water and applied to the wedding dress so as to bring purity in it, ritually. The corners of the clothes of bride and groom are being tied together in a knot as a sign of their oneness. Bride price is collected at the end or mid of every marriage. Raibaar and the parents of both boy and girl strictly follow each process of marriage as per their custom.

Phases in Bapla can be divided into different sections namely, Sar Sagun, Orah Duar Njel, Horah Chinah, Taka Chal and Newta.

Sar Sagun

(The initial proposal of marriage discussed by Raibaar with both the families)

In Sar Sagun, Raibaar take initiative to visit both families. He talks mostly with parents (if parents are dead, then head of the family) about the other family's interested in bride for their son/brother. Raibaar allow girl's family to have discussion with other family members. After few weeks or couple of day's times, if girl's family shows interest will inform Raibaar. So, that he can inform boy's family for the further processes.

Orah Duar Njel

(Parents and relatives of bride and groom visit each other's home)

If girl's family shows interest in the proposal put up by Raibaar. It means they are ready to go for further process, which is visiting to each other families. By visiting each other's families, they will not only examine the condition of living, status and other things but also check how the family members are and presenting themselves in front of other family

By visiting each other's families, they will not only examine the condition of living, status and other things but also check how the family members are and presenting themselves in front of other family members.

members. For that reason not only parents, relatives also visit to observation and discuss in various issues. After going back to respective home all family members come together and share point of their observation and all will give their opinion for the proposal.

But in most cases final decision is only depends on the parents of the boy or girl.

Horah Chinah

(Final decisions are taken by both the families and are conveyed by Raibaar)

After family has come to the final decision they will convey their decision through Raibaar. And it is his responsibility to convey other family. If the decision is negative, the process will end in this phase. If the decision is positive, the process will continue to next phase of marriage. Both parents will convey their decision to Majhi (headman of village) in order to get social sanctioned and involvement. It is rarely possible to arranged marriage without Majhi and villagers. Process also includes with substantiation by presenting cloths (most often) for to be bride and groom and the process is called Horoh Chinah.

Taka Chal

(Express decision to Manjhi (or Majhi) (headman of the village) and arrangement of marriage)

Parents will convey their decision of marriage to other family boy or girl by going to Majhi's home. After got confirmation from parents, Majhi call Jogmajhi and assign

> *Many customs are incomplete without the help of Majhi, Naike and Jogmajhi. And villagers play a vital role in helping in marriage's whole process.*

him to prepare for marriage. Majhi, Naike, Jogmajhi and villagers are also stake holders of marriage in village. Many customs are incomplete without the help of Majhi, Naike and Jogmajhi. And villagers play a vital role in helping in marriage's whole process. Taka Chal is the custom included with the process. In this process groom's family has to hand over meager money to bride's family.

Newta

(Invitation to relatives and final preparation of marriage)

After conveying decision of marriage to Headman, family members will be relaxed because they know the Majhi will take care of the customs and ceremonies. Family members will be busy inviting their relatives, friends, near and dear once. But first invitation is always to the Majhi.

Bapla

(The main ritual of Marriage)

Various categories of Bapla are as follows: Sangha Bapla (Ader bapla):

Sangha Bapla (Marriage) is referred to marriage done by elder brother's wife by younger brother in case of death and lost. It is common understanding between bride and groom side. Also need consent from wife of elder brother.

This marriage is done in order to prevent anyone from widowhood. Society accepts followed by some rituals and customs by more hor (five eminent people of village) villagers, naike and manjhi haram (headman). In brief it is required a man to become the husband of a deceased brother's widow.

Kirin Bapla is referred to purchase of 'would be bride' from her parent's home. In Sautari family, everyone in family contribute to occupation, which is agriculture.

Kadam Bapla

Kadam Bapla is generally done under kadam tree with all rituals and customs. This is oldest kind of marriage in Sautar community. In olden times, Sautars had no strong witness then nature. Kadam tree is useful and considered to be sacred in Sautar tradition. Now a day's even branch of Kadam tree is solving the problem—if kadam tree is not available.

Kirin Bapla

Kirin in Sautari means purchase. Kirin Bapla is referred to purchase of 'would be bride' from her parent's home. In Sautari family, everyone in family contribute to occupation, which is agriculture. Therefore, each family member is considered to be manpower. To compensate manpower one has to pay certain amount for bride to their parents. It is not considered to bride price but a customs for identify value of bride.

After finishing all customs bride sit inside decorated Rahi Chaudal to groom's house. Bride has to be taken only in Rahi Chaudal by the villagers/ relatives from groom's village.

Upagir Bapla

Sautar community is open towards interaction to male or female. Any male or female get along and come to common consent of getting marriage. Society accepts such kind of unionism and considered as marriage. It is without the information of parents but, later on parents are being informed by messenger of village i.e. assigned by Headman. Such kind of marriage occurs from haat (village, daily or weekly local market), pata (mela or community celebration of some occasion). There is special function for newly married couple called Tiril-Tarob. Where villagers have rights to ask and clear their doubt about both of them. This custom is done through a representative by headman. The entire question is being asked in indirect way to maintain the decorum of custom. Question like, have you ever married? Is being asked as "have you crossed anyone's barricade before?"

Tunki Dipil Bapla

This kind of bapla is also known as Rahi Chaudal Bapla (portable house for bride). After finishing all customs bride sit inside decorated Rahi Chaudal to groom's house. Bride has to be taken only in Rahi Chaudal by the villagers/ relatives from groom's village.

Itut-Sindur Bapla

Process of applying vermillion in mid of forehead of bride by the groom is called Itut. Usually the process is done in door of bride's home. This process is part and partial of marriage custom. And Itut custom is being done after completing certain years too.

Nirbelok Bapla

This kind of marriage is fixed in the childhood by parents. Nirbelok means who is not attended the age of adult.

Diku Bapla

Replicating Hindu methods of marriage or other than Sautar custom is called Diku Bapla. Diku in Sautar means outsider, term Diku was being used to denote British or any outsider in pre Independent India by Sautar Adivasi.

Haram Bariyat Bariyat

Haram mean old man in Sautar. Marriage led by Haram hor.

Sange Bariyat or Sange

Marriage accompanied by many.

Ghardi Jawain

In such marriages, groom is liable to stay in bride's house after marriage. This sort of marriage is mostly with single girl child family or elite Sautar family.

❑

5
Economic Livelihood

The Sautar population in Bihar lives in poverty stricken and backward areas resulting in scanty production and inadequate ecological resources. Indigenous knowledge is passed down from generation to generation and it provides a valuable resource for sustainable agricultural development. Economically, the Sautars may be described as plain agricultural type. The economy of the area can be best described as the one that operates at the subsistence level. The mode of production being primitive added with negligible marketable surplus, antiquated technology, high involvement of human labour and significant dependence on forest for food supply. Women play a very important role to significantly contribute in the tribal economy. They engross themselves in all domestic and agricultural activities.

In Bihar, Sautar's primary livelihood is agriculture. They also engage themselves in hunting and fishing. Agriculture practiced in the region is however predominantly rainfed

Over 80 percent of the total production of the region is cultivated during the Kharif season. Between June and November, the main crop cultivated is paddy. The growth of both early and late paddy variety occurs.

and only 14% of the area constitutes irrigated farming. 2.5 to 3 acre is the average size of the agricultural land holdings but in recent times, the productivity of most of the lands is low. June to September is the four months' time period when it rains and through this, irrigation purpose of the lands is served. The rainfall in the region varies from 1200 mm to 1300 mm. Multiple cropping is restricted as the intensity of rainfall is high and it is occurs for a relatively short time period.The present cropping pattern of Bihar is limited to cultivation of a single major kharif crop. Over 80 percent of the total production of the region is cultivated during the Kharif season. Between June and November, the main crop cultivated is paddy. The growth of both early and late paddy variety occurs. Lahvan is the early paddy variety which requires to be grown on highlands. On the other hand, Jarrhan, which is the late variety of paddy, needs high amount of soil moisture and has to be cultivated on lowlands. Maize and Madua are the two other important paddies grown alongside kharif crops.

Sarguja (mustard), an oilseed crop and wheat are the two major Rabi crops cultivated by the Sautars between September to January and end-November to April, respectively. Some farmers also grow Surthi, a local crop on the land getting heavy rainfall. Though, Sarguja has been replaced by mustard by most of the farmers keeping in mind its better quality of oil and higher produce.

Mixed cropping is practiced in this region. "In case of houses built on the farm lands, homestead agriculture for vegetable production is religiously practised and it is invariably the responsibility of the women member of the household to maintain the homestead farm. During the transect it was found that farmers leave aside small patches of land on which they grow multiple crops—beet root, raddish, black gram, tomatoes, potatoes, beans, onions etc. Most of these crops except for tomatoes and potatoes to an extent are grown for domestic consumption. The red variety such as kufri and sindri are susceptible to frost which is a common occurrence during the winter season. The white variety therefore has a higher yield owing to its ability to withstand frost and the area under white variety of potatoes is gradually increasing."

In raising the wheat crop, co-operative farming is practiced in the region. Though, due to various climatic disturbances and procedure mismanagement, cooperative farming often results in low productivity, farming proves to be advantageous for the local community under the present conditions because of low opportunity cost for labour in absence of alternate employment opportunities in the village and unavailability of adequate capital among the households for raising of the crops. The landless and marginal farmers are given an opportunity to participate and claim a share from the produce of cooperative farming. Unavailability of support irrigation facilities has been a major problem in the area. Later, with construction of check dams, percolation tanks and lift irrigation schemes the irrigation facilities of the Sautars. Assured water supply through lift irrigation schemes proved to be a boon. Many farmers were found to be putting increased area under tomato and potato crops which command a higher market price due to availability of support irrigation.

Forests are an integral part of the livelihood of the Sautars and it serves as a nucleus around which the economy and culture of the community revolves.

Forests are an integral part of the livelihood of the Sautars and it serves as a nucleus around which the economy and culture of the community revolves. The commonly found tree species in the forest are sal, mahua, teak, aamla, acacia species, harra and behra. The forests serve as an important source of fuel wood and virtually all the domestic fuel wood requirement in the household is met through the forests. Households often make piles of fuel wood procured from the forest outside their forest for later use. The fuel wood sourced from the forest is also an important source of income for the households. Bamboo is also commonly grown by most of the tribal households.

Apart from agriculture, food gathering and hunting are their important subsidiary occupations. Familiarity with animal husbandry contributes marginally to their livelihood. They fish in river, ponds andother water-logged areas with the help of nets, traps, bow and arrows. They also do fishing with the help of poisonous plants.

❑

6

Cultural Tradition

Performing Arts

Music

The Sautar music is characterised by simple tune and descending notes (from high pitch to low pitch). As music is not just an entertainment or luxury for the Sautars, their melody is very communicative. It is a part of their living. These re the common features of all tribal music. They are uncomplicated and effortless, narrating their day to day livelihood.

There are not more than two to three notations in their music and the tune remains the same, repeating itself in every line or paragraph with changed lyrics. The lyrics are mostly about the nature, festivals, rituals, agriculture, human emotions and simple conversations. Sautar music has a distinct intonation pattern, rhythmic structure and metrical mold as well as autonomous aesthetic, performativity

Sautar music has a distinct intonation pattern, rhythmic structure and metrical mold as well as autonomous aesthetic, performativity and transmission principles.

and transmission principles. Unthinking substitution of Sautar musical instruments by other instruments often leads to stark musical incompatibility.

The songs of Sautar are also an important part of their oral tradition. Some of the songs, mostly speaking of nature and its behaviour are:

Sedae ma dinre Jolomoy ma jugre
Candoe tahekana serma cetan Nutre tahe tahe
Kurha re tahe tahe Cando aris lena
Aris akan tey marsal keda

Long ago
The sun was above the sea in the sky The sun became angry
By living in the dark And by living in the fog His anger produced light.

Dakma cetan re Serma lata re Has hasi cerekin
Rak' homorok Tokarikin aboka Tokarikin japida
Has hasi cerekin udau langayen Thakurak bohok rikin aboka Onde gekin japida
Has hasi cerekin jiwetgeya

Water is above It is below the sky
The two, the Has and the Hasin weep Where will they sit ?

Where will they sleep?
The has and Hasin are not tired of flying They will sit on the head of god
They will sleep there
The two, the Has and the Hasin are alive !

Umin maran jolompjre Dak'ma talare
Pondge photo dombol dombol Nelkin mese daina Koyok kin me
Photo cetanre barya cerekin nelok kana

In the middle of water Of that very vast ocean
The white foam undulates, See O sister !
Look at the pair of birds Parching on it.

Tokoe ren co?
Sin cando ren kanae dak Nui phedok kan
Dak nu katet gecoy Ruar calak kan

The celestial horse of the day Descended on the sea from the sky
To whom this horse of gold belongs?
This belongs to the sun It descends to drink water
It returns after- drinkingwater.

Sermare dak banu Dhartire hasa
banu Sange dharti sajaw banu
Hoe doe rakap keda sermare dak
Lendon hasae rakap ket
Sangi dharti sajaw ena

There was no water in the sky.
There was no soil on the earth

Truly the earth was not fully arranged. The air lifted the water up into the sky. The female earthworm lifted the soil up Thus, the earth was properly arranged.

Laha pahil dharti losot ge Thol thole tahekan Cekate dharti rohor ena.
Losot' hawet lagit ponkhiraja Hoy may benaw ket Ona hadar hoy tege rohor ena

In the beginning The earth was marshy
How could the earth become dry?
To make the marshy land dry.
The Bird King created the air with that hard blowing air
It became dry

Tokoe jonom dharti Tokoe jonom pirthimi
Tokoe jonom dharti Manewa hor
Horo jonom dharti
Lendet ' jonom pirthimi H as-hasi cer ejonom
M anewa hor

From what did the earth originate? From what did the earth originate?
Form what did man of this earth originate ? This earth originated from the turtle The soil originated from the earthworm A pair of swans gave birth.

DANCE

Dance (enej) is an integral part of every celebration of the Sautar community. Both men and women dance in circular or semi-circular patterns in separate rows. Their arms are interlocked and they groove in clusters forming sequences.

Tamak, Tumdah, Juri Banam and Tiriya are the musical instruments which accompany the dance. Songs are sung while dancing by the dancers themselves.

Sautari dance is primarily performed on special occasions, especially during spring festival, accompanied by a traditional song.

Sautari dance is primarily performed on special occasions, especially during spring festival, accompanied by a traditional song. It often takes place within forested areas and depicts a kind of dedication to the forest Gods and Goddesses. It is also practiced to welcome guests.

The male dancers wear dhoti and turban, and decorate their bodies with branches of trees, leaves and flowers. Since the Sautars are believed to be close to nature, they use natural decors such as leaves, branches and flowers to do their make-up and design their clothes. The women dancers usually wear white or yellow sarees with red borders and adorn their hair with wild flowers. The length of the saree is about three inches above the heel. Flowers are tied around the bun which the women make.

Poush Parav dance, Maghe dance, Sarhuldance, Baha dance, Sarhul dance, Langrai dance, Dong dance, Gulwari dance, Sohrai dance, Dasai dance, Dansa dance, Dhonger dance, Morakaram dance and Singrai dance are performed during different occasions.

Poush Parav Dance: This dance is performed during the celebration of Poush, i.e, in the month of December-January, the harvest season. On the second day of Poush Parav the dancers are decked up as 'Buddhis Gadi' or Bahurupi. The boys of the community dress in girls' attire and roam from one house of the village to another. From every house, the dancers collect gifts. The whole celebration is incomplete without the dance of Poush Parav.

Baha Dance: The word 'Baha' literally means flower.

Baha Parab is celebrated by the Sautars welcoming the advent of Spring, when fresh flowers and leaves grow on trees. The flower of Sal tree is considered sacred and the tree is specially worshipped. Both men and women dance to the beats of drum for three days. The first day is known as 'Nayake Maha' or Priest Day. The second day is termed as 'Serva Maha' and the third day as 'Rasca Maha' or the Day of Enjoyment. Women tug fresh flowers and leaves of Sal and Mahua tree, in their hair.

Maghe Dance: Maghe is a ritualistic dance performed

to evoke Goddess Dasauli, who lives in the grove of Sal trees. It is performed during the celebration of Maghe Parav where the people dance all night long.

Good harvest and advent of spring is celebrated in the dance. Women and men together dance to the joyous music expressing their love and attachment to nature.

Dong Dance: Dong is performed by the Sautar women singing to the tune and accompanied by male members in musical instrument. This dance is specifically performed during the marriage ceremony, wishing good luck to the newly married couple and also praying for their good health and prosperity.

Gulwari Dance: Gulwari dance is performed by the females of the Sautar community accompanied by the males in music. During Sarhul, the dancers dance along the village roads. Whenever they reach a crossroad, they pause to perform Gulwari dance. The theme of the songs are related to nature, environment and simple interactions.

Sohrai Dance: Sohrai is a celebration for bounty agricultural harvest and also domestication of cow. The ceremony is celebrated a day after Diwali and cows are offered prayers to mark the occasion. On this ritualistic day, the painting practiced is called Sohrai dance, hence the nomenclature. The women of the tribe perform Sohrai dance.

Dasai Dance: Dasai dance is performed during the religious festival – Durga Puja. The dance recites the story of how Devi and Durga rescued Alom and Kajol from the hands of the Kidnappers. Dasai Parab recalls the whole incident of the search and rescue of the two abducted mythical characters by the powerful Devi and Durga. The parab ends on the same day of Vijay Dashami. This dance is performed by the men who dress like women. They adorn their turbans with peacock feathers. The women offer handful of grains to the dancers as a mark of appreciation.

Sarhul Dance: The Sarhul dance are performed on the occasion of Sarhul festival, by the tribe accompanied by the songs which narrates the stories related to culture, beliefs and tradition of the tribe. Sarhul festival marks the beginning of New Year. Celebrated every year in the first month of the Hindu calendar, on the third day of the moon or the fortnight of 'Chaitra', Sarhul marks the advent of the spring season or "Phaagun" and is celebrated till the month of June or "Jeth".

Langrai Dance: There is no specific occassion to perform the Langrai dance. The women perform accompanied by music played by men to celebrate any festival or mark the commencement of any ceremony. 'Majithan' is a religious place of the Sautars where various rituals are performed. Langrai can only be performed on the sacred spot.

Dansa Dance: Dansa narrates the myth of birth, life and death of the Sautar community. Through the dance, mythical stories are unfolded. The male members perform Dansa as they recite the story of ancestral myth through their song.

Dhonger Dance: Dhonger is the hunting (Shikari) dance of Sautars. The men, through this dance depict their hunting skills and the story of entering the jungle to hunt and bring prey home. Once the hunt is over and brought home, celebration follows and all members engage in rejoicing the moment.

Morakaram Dance: Morakaram is performed by the men of the Sautar community when demise of any member occurs. This dance is dedicated to the departed souls, offering prayers to them. The whole village participates in the mourning and recalls the good deed of the departed soul.

MUSICAL INSTRUMENTS

Tamak

Tamak is a percussion instrument of the Sautar community of Bihar. The base structure of the instrument is from mud. The mud is given a semicircular structure and burnt to make

it strong enough as desired to make the instrument. The open mouth of the base structure is covered with leather of cow's skin. The diameter of the instrument measures about 1.5 feet. The leather plat on the mouth is fixed to the base with the help of strings made from cow's skin. This holds the leather taut and suitable for the music that it will produce. Mala Kanthi is used to play to this percussion instrument.

Dhaak

Dhaak is a percussion musical instrument of Sautar community of Jharkhand. It is usually made of wood but nowadays for making of the instrument easier, steel metal is also used to make the structure of the Dhaak. It is a bi-facial musical instrument having a lenght of 4 feet and 3 inches. Both the faces of the instrument are covered with leather. The left mouth is broader than the right. The diameter of the left face is 1 feet and 5 inches and the diameter of the right face is 10 inches.

Tumdah

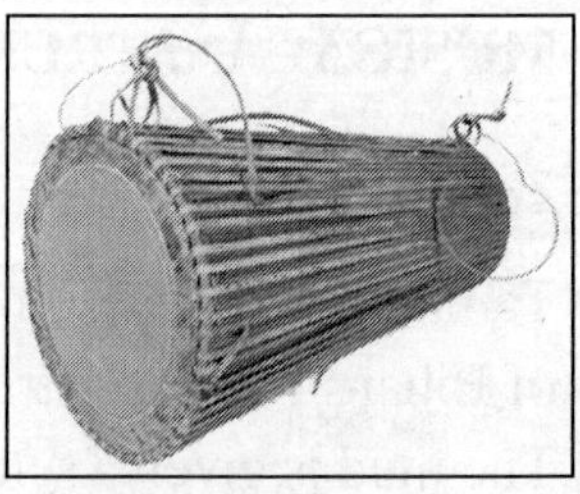

The structure of Tumdah is made of burnt clay. It is cylindrical in shape with left side being wider than right. This hollow shape is tapered from left to right decreasingly. Bullock skin is used for covering the left side and the goat skin is used for covering the right side. Single instrument is played by one man. This instrument is used at all social events except during the death rituals.

Juri Banam

Juri Banam is one of the traditional instruments of the Sautar community as well as one of the revered instruments. Banam can either be made from a solid wooden block or can be prepared by joining different parts. Banam made of wooden is broader at one end and narrower at the other end. The narrower side is used as handle. Threads made of long hairs of horse are used to join both the ends. The broader end is made hollow and covered with thin leather. A stick is tied with the horse hair thread to make a small bow and is held in right hand.

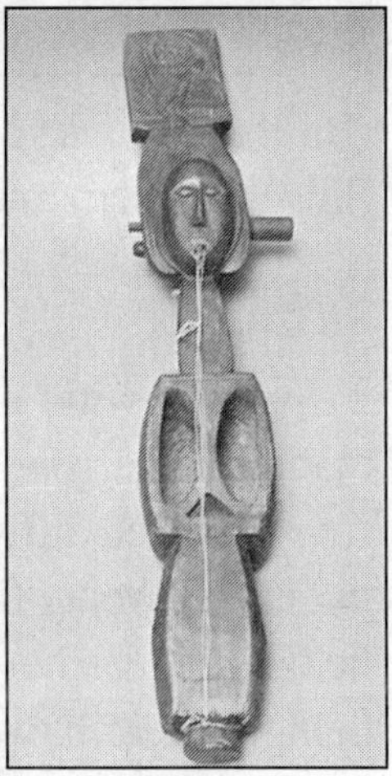

The wooden part is held in left side and it is played with the string held in right hand. Salga gum is pasted at the side of the wooden part which is applied to the threads of horse hair for generating necessary friction. Coconut shell is also used as substitute to the wooden block.

Sakna

Singa is a wind musical instrument of the Sautar community of Bihar. The horn of the buffalo is used to make the instrument. The components inside the horn are cleaned. The tribal community plays this instrument by blowing

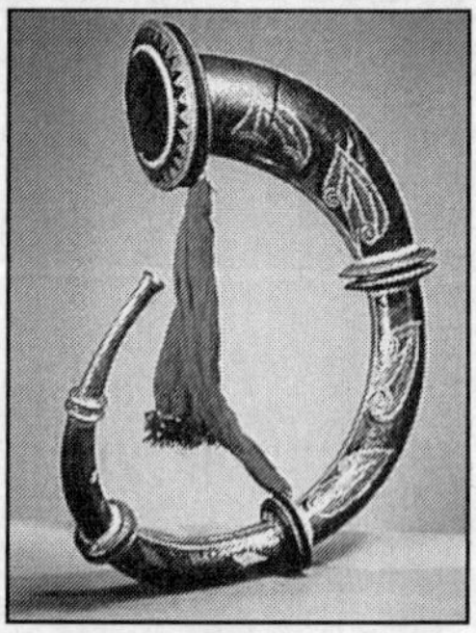

wind from the narrow end of the horn. Traditionally, Singa was taken as a heroic instrument played during military practices. Now, the tribal community blows in happiness to celebrate while dancing. Singa is also found in other states with different names and sizes such as Shinga (Bhills), Kohuk (Madhya Pradesh), Reliki (Northern East), Singa (Odisha) and Pepa (Assam).

Tiriyo

Tiriyo is a wind musical instrument of the Sautars. This is made of a narrow hollow bamboo. Its best size ranges from four hundred fifty to six hundred fifty mm in length and twenty to twenty five mm in diameter. Both or one side may be open. A Tiriyo has five circular holes on the surface one being for air blowing purpose and the other four (closely situated) for controlling the flow of air for different notes.

ORAL LITERATURE

Sautari Songs

Dong Song is sung specially during marriage occasions and Chaitihar (Naming of Children)

Da talang daka talang
Jhumur baihad rin haku talang Adhan dolang raase ko
aa Adhan dolang tase ko aa Naase naase dolang jojo

aako Jil kuti kuti Sodom Sibil ge njodom
njodomSidup aate jom ge raase Sodom
Taati jhari Gada Gelej kunj daLuy luybin kudinj dipil
aabin Alinj tilinj luy aa
Alinj tilinj dipil aa
Aam do menay tama kirinj rani Abin ge juri kudi
Latar sene hoy jaapud ked Benaw alanj
Thok thuki thok do
Hoyte ada lipi
Hoyte Palen otang aa
Benaw alang lipi chaatom ada .
Buru khoninj aandgo len do
Tikin re baad baha njur akaan do
Halang haling tege
Gocha gocha tege

SAUTAR FOLK-TALES

The Magic Lamp

In the capital of a certain raja, there lived a poor widow. She had an only son who was of comely form and handsome countenance. One day a merchant from a far country came to her house, and standing in front of the door called out, "Dada, Dada," (elder brother). The widow replied, "He is no more, he died many years ago." On hearing this the merchant wept bitterly, mourning the loss of his younger brother. He remained some days in his sister-in-law's house, at the end of which he said to her, "This lad and I will go in quest of the golden flowers, prepare food for our journey." Early next morning they set out taking provisions with them for the way. After they had gone a

They had no fire with them, but the merchant ordered his nephew to blow with his mouth as if he were kindling the embers of a fire.

considerable distance, the boy being fatigued said, “Oh! uncle I can go no further.” The merchant scolded him, and walked along as fast as he could. After some time the boy again said, “I am so tired I can go no further.” His uncle turned back and beat him, and he, nerved by fear, walked rapidly along the road. At length they reached a hill,to the summit of which they climbed, and gathered a large pile of firewood. They had no fire with them, but the merchant ordered his nephew to blow with his mouth as if he were kindling the embers of a fire. He blew until he was exhausted, and then said, “What use is there in blowing when there is no fire?” The merchant replied “Blow, or I shall beat you.” He again blew with all his might for a short time, and then stopping, said, “There is no fire, how can it possibly burn?” on which the merchant struck him. The lad then redoubled his efforts, and presently the pile of firewood burst into a blaze. On the firewood being consumed, an iron trap-door appeared underneath the ashes, and the merchant ordered his nephew to pull it up. He pulled,but finding himself unable to open it, said, “It will not open.” The merchant told him to pull with greater force, and he, being afraid lest he should be again beaten, pulled with all his might, but could not raise it. He again said, “It will not open,” whereupon the merchant struck him, and ordered him to try again. Applying himself with all his might, he at length succeeded. On the door being raised, they saw a lamp burning, and beside it an immense quantity of golden flowers.

A ring, which he wore on his finger, came into contact with the lamp, and immediately a fairy issued from it, and asked, "What is it you want with me?"

The merchant then said to the boy, "As you enter do not touch any of the gold flowers, but put out the lamp, and heap on the gold tray as many of the gold flowers as you can, and bring them away with you." He did as he was ordered, and on reaching the door again requested his uncle to relieve him of the gold flowers, but he refused, saying, "Climb up as best as you can." The boy replied, "How can I do so, when my hands are full?" The merchant then shut the iron trap door on him, and went away to a distant country.

The boy being imprisoned in the dark vault, wept bitterly, and having no food, in a few days he became very weak. Taking the lamp in his hand, he sat down in a corner, and without knowing what he was doing, began to rub the lamp with his hand. A ring, which he wore on his finger, came into contact with the lamp, and immediately a fairy issued from it, and asked, "What is it you want with me?" He replied, "Open the door and let me out." The fairy opened the door, and the boy went home taking the lamp with him. Being hungry, he asked for food, but his mother replied, "There is nothing in the house that I can give you." He then went for his lamp, saying, "I will clean it, and then sell it,

When the boy had become a young man, it so happened, that one day the raja's daughter was being carried to the ghat to bathe, and he seeing her palki with the attendants passing, went to his mother and said, "I am going to see the princess."

and with the money buy food." Taking the lamp in his hand he began to rub it, and his ring again touching it, a fairy issued from it and said "What do you wish for?" The boy said, "Cooked rice and uncooked rice." The fairy immediately brought him an immense quantity of both kinds of rice. Sometime after this, certain merchants brought horses for sale, and the boy seeing them wished to buy one. Having no money, he remembered his lamp, and taking it up, pressed his ring against it, and the fairy instantly appeared, and asked him what he wanted. He said, "Bring me a horse," and immediately the fairy presented to him an immense number of horses.

When the boy had become a young man, it so happened, that one day the raja's daughter was being carried to the ghat to bathe, and he seeing her palki with the attendants passing, went to his mother and said, "I am going to see the princess." She tried to dissuade him, but he insisted on her giving him permission, so at length she gave him leave. He went secretly, and saw her as she was bathing, and on returning home, said to his mother, "I have seen the princess, and I am in love with her. Go, and inform the raja that your son loves his daughter, and begs her hand in marriage." His mother said, "Do you think the raja will consider us as on equality with him?" He would not, however, he kept urging her daily to carry his message to the raja, until she being wearied with his importunity went to the palace, and on being admitted to an audience, informed the raja that her son was enamoured of the princess, his daughter, and begged that she might be given to him in marriage. The raja made answer that on her son giving him a large sum of money which he named, and which would have been beyond the means of the raja himself, he would be prepared to give his daughter in marriage to her son. The young man then recourse to his lamp and ring, and the fairy supplied him with a much larger sum of money than the raja had demanded. He took it all,and gave it to the raja, who was astonished beyond measure at the sight of such immense wealth. After a reasonable time the old mother was sent to the raja to request him to fulfill his promise, but he, being reluctant to see his daughter united to one so much her inferior in station, in hope of being relieved from the obligation to fulfill his promise, demanded that a palace suited to her rank and station in life be prepared for her, after which he would no longer delay the nuptials. The would-be bridegroom applied to his never failing friends, his lamp and ring, and on the fairy appearing begged him to build a large castle in one night, and to furnish and adorn it as befitted the residence of a raja's daughter. The fairy complied with the request, and the whole city was amazed

When the raja and his son-in-law returned from the chase, they were surprised and alarmed to find that the palace with its fair occupant has vanished, and hadn't left a trace behind.

next morning at the sight of a lordly castle,where the evening before there had not been even a hut. The dewan tried to dissuade the raja, but without effect, and in due time the marriage was celebrated amid great rejoicings.

On a certain day, sometime after the marriage, the raja and his son-in-law went to the forest to hunt. During their absence, the merchant to whom reference has already been made, arrived at the castle gate, bearing in his hand a new lamp which he offered in exchange to the princess for any old lamp she might possess. She thought it a good opportunity to obtain a new lamp in place of her husband's old one and without knowing what she did, gave the magic lamp to the merchant,and received a new one in return. The merchant rubbed his ring on the magic lamp, and the fairy obeyed the summons, and desired to know what he wanted. He said, "Convey the castle as it stands with the princess in it, to my own country," and instantly his wish was gratified.

When the raja and his son-in-law returned from the chase, they were surprised and alarmed to find that the palace with its fair occupant has vanished, and hadn't left a trace behind. The dewan reminded his master that he had tried to dissuade him from rashly giving his daughter in marriage to an unknown person, and had foretold that some calamity was sure to follow. The raja being grieved and angry at the loss of his daughter, sent for her husband, and said to him, "I give you thirteen days during which to find my daughter. If you fail, on the morning of the fourteenth, I shall surely cause you to be executed." The thirteenth day arrived, and although her husband had sought her everywhere, the princess had not been found. Her unhappy husband resigned himself to his fate, saying, "I shall go and rest, tomorrow morning I shall be killed." So he climbed to the top of a high hill, and lay down to sleep upon a rock. At noon he accidentally rubbed his finger ring upon the rock on which he lay, and a fairy issued from it, and awaking him, demanded what he wanted. In reply he said, "I have lost my wife and my palace,if you know where they are, take me to them." The fairy immediately transported him to the gate of his castle in the merchant's country,and then left him to his own devices. Assuming the form of a dog, he entered the palace, and the princess at once recognized him. The merchant had gone out on business, and had taken the lamp with him, suspended by a chain around his neck. After consultation, it was determined that the princess should put poison in the merchant's food that

Assuming the form of a dog, he entered the palace, and the princess at once recognized him. The merchant had gone out on business, and had taken the lamp with him, suspended by a chain around his neck.

evening. When he returned, he called for his supper, and the princess set before him the poisoned rice, after eating which he quickly died. The rightful owner repossessed himself of the magic lamp, and an application of the ring brought out the attendant fairy who demanded to know why he had been summoned.

"Transport my castle with the princess and myself in it back to the king's country, and place it where it stood before," said the young man; and instantly the castle occupied its former position. So that before the morning of the fourteenth day dawned, not only had the princess been found,but her palace had been restored to its former place. The raja was delighted at receiving his daughter back again. He divided his kingdom with his son-in-law, giving him one-half, and they ruled the country peacefully and prosperously for many years.

The Two Brothers, Jhorea, and Jhore

There were two brothers, whose parents died, leaving them orphans when very young. The name of the elder was Jhorea, and of the younger Jhore. On the death of their parents, the two brothers went to seek employment, which they found in a certain village, far from where their home had been. The elder, Jhorea, was engaged as a farm servant,and the younger, Jhore, as village goat-herd.

After some time, it so happened that one day the brothers had no rice for their dinner, and Jhorea said to his brother, "Go to the owners of the goats you herd, and ask them for the hire they promised you. One will give you a pai, another a pawa, and a third a paila, and soon, according to the number of animals they have in your charge; some will give you more and others less, bring what you get, and cook some for dinner." The boy went as he was ordered, and entering the first house he came to, said, "Give me a pai." They said, "What do you want with a pai?" "Never mind what I want with it, give it,"he replied. So they gave him a pai. Then he went to another house and said, "Give me a pawa." "What do you want with a pawa?" they said.

"Never you mind, give it to me," and they gave him a pawa. He then went to a third house and asked for a paila. "What do you want with a paila?" they enquired.

"Never you mind, give it to me," and they gave him a pawa. He then went to a third house and asked for a paila. "What do you want with a paila?" they enquired. "Nevermind, give it to me," he replied. Instead of bringing rice he brought the wooden measures, and breaking them into small pieces, put them into the pot to cook. The elder brother was ploughing, and being very hungry, he kept calling out, "Cook the rice quickly, cook the rice quickly." Finding his brother being impatient, he stirred the contents of the pot with all his might, at the same time exclaiming, "What can be the matter brother? It is very hard." The elder brother came to see what was wrong, and on looking into the pot saw only pieces of wood. He became very angry, and said, "I sent you to bring rice, why did you bring measures?" To which he replied, "You told me to ask a pai from one, a pawa from another, and a paila from a third, and I did so."

The elder then said to the younger, "You go and plough, and if the plough catch in a root on the right hand, cut the root on the left hand, and if it catch in a root on the left side, cut the root on the right side, and in the meantime I will cook." He went and began to plough, and in a short time the plough caught in a root on the right, and not understanding the directions given to him, he struck the left hand bullock a blow on the leg with his axe. The bullock limped along a short distance. When the plough caught in a root on the left, he smote the bullock on the right, wounding it as he had done the other. Both of the bullocks then lay down, and although he beat them they did not get up. He therefore called to his brother, "These bullocks have lain down, and will not get up, what I shall do?" "Beat them," was the reply. Again he beat them, but with no better results. The elder brother then came, and found that the oxen had been maimed, and were unable to stand, at which he became greatly alarmed, and said, "Why did you maim the oxen? The owners will beat us to death today." He then gave him some parched grain to eat,and sent him to look after his goats. The sun being hot, the goats were lying in the shade chewing their cud. He sat down near them, and began to eat the parched grain. Seeing the goats moving their jaws as if eating, he said, "These goats are eating nothing, they are lying there mocking me," and becoming enraged, he killed the mall with his axe. Then going to his brother, he said,

"Oh! brother,I have killed all the goats." His brother asked, "Why did you kill them?" He replied, "While I was watching them and eating the parched grain which you gave me, I saw them chewing, and as they were eating nothing I knew they were mocking me, and so I killed them all." The elder brother became greatly alarmed, and call the younger to come, they quickly ate their dinner, and then went to where the goats were lying dead. From among them they chose the fattest, and carried it off to the jungle, where they flayed, and cut it into pieces.

"While I was watching them and eating the parched grain which you gave me, I saw them chewing, and as they were eating nothing I knew they were mocking me, and so I killed them all."

Jhore then said, "I shall take the stomach as my share," but his brother said, "No, let us take the flesh." Jhore, however, would not agree to that, and at length his brother said, "Well you take the stomach, I shall take the flesh." So each took what he fancied most, and they set off. After travelling a long distance, they came to a large tree growing on the side of the road, onto which they climbed for safety. After they had been sometime on the tree, a raja on his way to be married, lay down to rest in its shade, and when he and his attendants had fallen asleep, Jhore let the goat's stomach fall down on the raja. The raja having his rest thus rudely disturbed, sprang to his feet, and calling out, awoke

While walking about in the jungle, they collected bees, wasps, and other stinging insects, and put them into the drum.

his servants, who seeing the goat's stomach, and not knowing what had happened, thought the raja himself had burst. They fled in terror followed by the raja, and did not halt till they were many miles away from the scene of the raja's discomfiture.

After waiting a little while, the brothers descended, and began to help themselves to the raja's property. Jhore said, "I shall take the drum." His brother said, "No, let us take the brass vessels and the clothes." Jhore, however, insisted, and after considerable wrangling, his brother said, "Well, take the drum if you will have it, I shall take the brass vessels and the clothes." So each took what pleased him best, and then they went away and hid in the jungle.

While walking about in the jungle, they collected bees, wasps, and other stinging insects, and put them into the drum. Having filled the drum, they emerged from the forest at a place where a washerman was washing clothes. Jhore tore all his clothes into strips, and scattered them about. The washerman went and told the raja that two persons had come out from the jungle, and had destroyed all his clothes. On hearing this, the raja said to his servants, "Come, and let us fight with these two men." So arming themselves with guns, they went to the tank where Jhorea and Jhore were sitting, and began to shoot at them, but the bullets did them no harm. When their ammunition was exhausted,they said,

"Will you still fight?" The brothers answered, "Yes, we will fight." So they began to fire their guns, and beat their drum,and the bees and wasps issued from it like a rope, and began to sting the raja and his soldiers, who to save themselves, lay down and rolled on the ground. The raja, in anguish from the stings of the bees, exclaimed, "I will give you my daughter, and half of my kingdom, if you will call off the bees." Hearing this they beat the drum,and calling to the bees and wasps, ordered them all to enter the drum again, and the raja and his people went to their homes. The brothers however, could not agree as to who should marry the princess. One said, "You marry her." The other said, "No, you marry her." The younger at length said to the elder, "You are the elder; you should take her, as it is not fitting that you should be begging. If I were to marry her, I could no longer go about begging." So the elder brother married the princess, and became the raja's son-in-law.

The two settled down there, and cultivated all kinds of crops. One day the elder brother sent his younger brother to bring a certain kind of grain. Taking a sickle and a rope to tie his sheaves with, he went to the field. Arriving

The two settled down there, and cultivated all kinds of crops. One day the elder brother sent his younger brother to bring a certain kind of grain. Taking a sickle and a rope to tie his sheaves with, he went to the field.

> *On being informed of his brother's action, Jhorea seized a stick, and ran after him to beat him, but could not overtake him. In the direction Jhore was running, there were some men flaying an ox.*

there, he found that the grain was covered with insects. So he set fire to it and while it was burning he kept calling out, "Whoever desires to feast on roasted insects, let him come here." When his brother knew what he had done, he reprimanded him severely.

Some time afterwards, when the black rice was ripe, he again ordered him to go and reap some, so getting a sickle, and rope to bind his sheaves with, he went to the rice field. On looking about to see where he would begin, he discovered that each stalk of rice was covered with flies. "There is nothing here but flies. How can I reap this?" Saying this, he set fire to the growing rice and burnt it all to the ground. His brother, when he knew what had happened, was very much displeased and threatened to beat him.

On another day he was sent to cut jari to make ropes, so taking his sickle, he set off to the field of jari. As soon as he began to cut the stalks, the seeds rattled in the pods, hearing which he stopped and called out, "Who is calling me?" After listening a while and hearing nothing he began again, and the same noise issuing from the plant he was cutting, he said, "These plants are remonstrating with me for cutting them." So being offended, he set fire to and burnt down the whole crop of jari.

On being informed of his brother's action, Jhorea seized a stick, and ran after him to beat him, but could not overtake him. In the direction Jhore was running, there were some men flaying an ox, and Jhorea called to them to lay hold of his brother. They could not, however, accomplish this, but as he passed, they threw the stomach of the ox at him, which he caught in his arms and carried away with him. Finding a drain that was open at both ends, he crept in at one end, and passed out at the other, but left the ox's stomach behind him. His brother soon arrived at the drain, and thinking he was still there, tried to drive him out by pushing in a stick, the sharp point of which perforated the ox's stomach. On withdrawing the stick, and seeing the contents of the ox's stomach adhering to it, he thought he had pierced and killed his brother, but he having passed out at the other end had run swiftly home, and hid himself among the rafters of the house. Jhorea returned home weeping, and immediately began to make the preparations necessary for Jhore's funeral ceremonies. He caused a sumptuous feast to be got ready, and invited all his relations and friends. When they were all assembled, he went into the house to offer Jhore his portion. Presenting it, he said, "Oh! My brother Jhore, I offer this to you, take it, and eat it." Jhore, from among the rafters said, "Give it to me brother, and I shall eat it." His brother, not expecting an answer, was alarmed, and fled to his friends without,exclaiming, "Do the spirits of dead men speak? Jhore's speaks."

When day began to dawn, Jhore's tiger evinced a tendency to leave the road and take to the jungle, but Jhore holding him in, exclaimed, "Ha! Ha! My Hindu steed. Ha! ha! My Hindu steed."

It now being dark, Jhore descended from his perch, and taking up the food which had been cooked for his funeral feast, left the house by another door. Passing on to the high way, he kept calling out, "Travellers by the road or dwellers in the jungle, if you require food, come here." Some thieves hearing him, said, "Come, and let us go and ask some." So going to him they said, "Give us some too, Jhore." But he replied, "It is for me alone." On their asking a second time,he gives it to them. After they had eaten it all, they said to him, "Come, and let us go thieving." So they went to a house, and while the thieves were searching for money, Jhore went and picked up small pieces of pottery, and tied them up in his cloth. When they met afterwards, seeing Jhore's bundle of what appeared like rupees, they said, "You were not with us, where did you get the money?" Opening his parcel, he showed them the pieces of pottery, seeing which they said, "We will not have you as our comrade." He replied, "Then return the food which you ate." As they could not comply, they agreed to take him with them. Jhore then said, "Where shall we go now?" They replied, "To steal cloth." So they went to a house, and while the robbers were searching for cloth, Jhore began to pull the clothes from off the sleeping inmates. This awoke them, and starting up, they began to call loudly for help. The thieves made off, and Jhore with them. Seeing Jhore had spoiled their game, they said to him, "We will not allow you to go with us again." He said, "Then give me back the food you ate." Not being able to do so, they said, "Well, we will allow you to accompany us this once." Jhore then said, "What shall we steal now?" The thieves answered, "We shall now go to steal horses." So they went to a stable, and each of the thieves helped himself to a horse; but Jhore going behind the house, found a large tiger which he saddled and mounted. The thieves also mounted each on the horse they had stolen. As they rode along, Jhore's tiger sometimes went first,and sometimes the thieves' horses. When the thieves were in front, Jhore's tiger bit and scratched their horses, so they said to him, "You ride first, we shall follow." But Jhore said, "No, my horse is a Hindu horse, he cannot run in front, your horses are Sautar horses, they run well and straight, so you ride ahead." When day began to dawn, Jhore's tiger evinced a tendency to leave the road and take to the jungle, but Jhore holding him in, exclaimed, "Ha! Ha! My Hindu steed. Ha! ha! My Hindu steed." When it was fully light, the tiger ran into the jungle, and Jhore got caught in the branch of a tree,and continued dangling there for some days.

It so happened that one morning a demon passing that way spied Jhore dangling from the tree, and seizing him, put him in a bag and carried him away. Being thirsty, he laid the bag down, and went to a spring to drink. While

While he was absent, Jhore got out of the bag, and putting a stone in instead, ran away. The demon having quenched his thirst, returned, and lifting the bag carried it home.

he was absent, Jhore got out of the bag, and putting a stone in instead, ran away. The demon having quenched his thirst, returned, and lifting the bag carried it home. His daughter came to welcome him, and he said to her, "Jhore is in the bag, cook him, and we shall have a feast." He then went to invite his friends to share it with him. When the demon's daughter had opened the bag, she found the stone, and was angry, because her father had deceived her. In a short time her father returned, bringing a large number of jackals with him. He said to her, "Have you cooked Jhore?" She replied, "Tush! tush! You brought me a stone."

The demon was highly incensed at having been outwitted, and exclaimed, "I will track Jhore until I find him, and this time I shall bring him home without laying him down." He then left, and before long found Jhore swinging in the same branch as before. Catching hold of him, he put him into a bag, the mouth of which he tied. This time he brought him home without once laying him down. Calling to his daughter, he said, "Cook Jhore, while I go to invite my friends." She untied the bag, and took Jhore out, and seeing his long hair, she said, "How is it that your hair has grown so long?" "I pounded it in the dhenki," he replied. "Will you pound mine, so that it may become long like yours," said the demon's daughter. Jhore replied, "I shall do so with pleasure, put your head in the dhenki, and I shall pound it." So she put in her head, and he pounded it so that he killed her. He then possessed himself of all her jewellery, and dressing in her clothes, cooked her body.

When the demon returned, accompanied by his friends, he said, "Well! daughter, have you cooked Jhore?" Jhore replied, "Yes, I have cooked him." On hearing this, the demon and the jackals, who had come with him, were delighted, and setting to, they devoured the body of the demon's daughter.

After some days, the demon went to visit a friend, and Jhore divesting himself of the demon girl's clothes, went to where the demon had at first found him, and began to swing as before. Presently a tigress approached him and said, "Oh! Brother, the hair of my cubs have grown very long, I wish you to shave them today." Jhore replied, "Oh! Sister, boils some water, and then goes to the spring to bring more." The tigress having boiled the water went to the spring.

While she was away, Jhore poured the boiling water over the two cubs, and scalded them to death.

After some days, the demon went to visit a friend, and Jhore divesting himself of the demon girl's clothes, went to where the demon had at first found him, and began to swing as before.

He made them grin by fixing the lips apart, and propped them up at the door of the tigress' house. On her return as she drew near, she saw her cubs, as she fancied, laughing, and said to herself. "They are delighted because their uncle has shaved them." Setting down her water pot, she went to look at them, and found them dead. Just then the demon came up, and she asked him, "Whom are you seeking today uncle?" He replied "I am seeking Jhore, he has caused me to eat my own daughter. Whom are you seeking?" The tigress replied, "I also am seeking Jhore; he has scalded my cubs to death."

The two then went in search of Jhore. They found him in a lonely part of the forest preparing birdlime, and said to him, "What are you doing, Jhore?" He replied, "I look high up, and then I look deep down." They said, "Teach us to do it too." He answered, "Only I can do it." They asked him a second time, and received the same reply. On their begging him a third time to teach them, he said, "Well, I shall do it." He then put some of the birdlime into their eyes, and fixed their eyelids together, so that they could not open them. While they were washing their eyes, he ran away. As soon as they had rid themselves of the birdlime, they followed him and found him distilling oil from the fruit of the marking-nut tree. They said to him, "What are you doing, Jhore?" He replied, "I look deep down, and then high up." They said,"Teach us also." He replied, "Only I can do it." They asked him again, and he said, "Well I will do it." He then poured some of the oil he had distilled into their eyes. It burned them so, that they became stone-blind.

Jhore was next seen seated in a fig-tree eating the fruit. Some cattle merchants, passing under the tree with a large herd of cattle, saw him eating the figs, and asked him what it was he was eating. He replied, "Beat the bullock that is going last, and you shall find it." So they beat the bullock till it fell down. In the meantime, the herd had gone on ahead, and Jhore running after them drove them to his own house. His brother seeing the large herd of cattle, asked to whom they belonged. Jhore replied, "They are Jhore's property." Jhorea then said, "I killed my brother Jhore, which Jhore is it?" He made answer, "Your brother Jhore whom you thought you had killed." Jhorea was delighted to find his brother alive, and said to him, "Let us live together after this." So they lived peacefully together ever after.

Some cattle merchants, passing under the tree with a large herd of cattle, saw him eating the figs, and asked him what it was he was eating. He replied, "Beat the bullock that is going last, and you shall find it."

The Boy and his Stepmother

A certain boy had charge of a cow which he used to tend while grazing. One day the cow said to him, "How is it that you are becoming so emaciated?" The boy replied, "My stepmother does not give me sufficient food." The

The next day they proceeded to make arrangements to kill the cow, and finding the rope prepared by the boy the day before, they tied her with it to a stake.

cow then said to him, "Do not tell anyone, and I will give you food. Go to the jungle and get leaves with which to make a plate and cup." The boy did as he was ordered, and behold, the cow from one horn shook boiled rice into the leaf plate, and from the other a relish for the rice into the cup. This continued daily for a considerable time, until the boy became sleek and fat.

The stepmother came to know of the relation which existed between the cow and her herd-boy, and to be revenged upon them she feigned illness. To her attendants she said, "I cannot possibly live." They asked, "What would make you live?" She replied, "If you kill the cow, I will recover." They said, "If killing the cow will cure you, we will kill it." The boy hearing that the life of the cow which supplied him with food was threatened, ran to her and said, "They are about to kill you." Hearing this the cow said, "You go and make a rope of rice straw, make some parts thick, and some thin, and put it in such a place as they can easily find it. When they are about to kill me, you seize hold of my tail and pull." The next day they proceeded to make arrangements to kill the cow, and finding the rope prepared by the boy the day before, they tied her with it to a stake. After she was tied the boy take hold of her tail, and pulled so that the rope by which she was secured was made slack. A man now raised an axe, and felled her by a blow on the forehead. As the cow staggered the rope broke, and she and the boy were borne away with the wind, and alighted in an unexplored jungle. From the one cow other cows sprang, in number equal to a large herd, and from them another large herd was produced. The boy then drove his two herds of cows to a place where they could graze, and afterwards took them to the river to drink. The cows having quenched their thirst, lay down to rest, and the boy bathed, and afterwards combed and dressed his hair. During this latter operation a hair from his head fell into the river, and was carried away by the current.

Some distance lower down, a princess with her female companions and attendants came to bathe. While the princess was in the water she noticed the hair floating down stream, and ordered someone to take it out, which when done they measured, and found it to be twelve cubits long. The princess on returning home went to the king, her father, and showing him the hair she had found in the river said, "I have made up my mind to marry the man to whom this hair belonged." The king gave his consent, and commanded his servants to search for the object of his daughter's affection.

The king's servants after a long consultation as to whom they should next apply to, decided upon laying the matter before a tame parrot belonging to the king.

They having received the king's command went to a certain barber and said to him, "You dress the hair and beards of all the men in this part of the country, tell us where the man with hair twelve cubits long is to be found." The barber, after many days, returned unsuccessful. The king's servants after a long consultation as to whom they should next apply to, decided upon laying the matter before a tame parrot belonging to the king. Going to the parrot they said, "Oh parrot, can you find the man whose hair is twelve cubits long?" The parrot replied, "Yes, I can find him." After flying here and there the parrot was fortunate enough to find the boy. It was evening, and having driven his two herds of cattle into their pen, he had sat down, and was employed in dressing his long hair. His flute was hanging on a bush by his side.

The parrot sat awhile considering how she might take him to the king's palace. Seeing the flute the idea was suggested to her, that by means of it she might contrive to lead him where she desired. So taking it up in her beak, she flew forward a little and alighted in a small bush. To regain possession of his flute the boy followed, but on his approach the bird flew away, and alighted on another bush a short distance ahead. In this way she continued to lead him by flying from bush to bush until at length she brought him to the king's palace. He was then brought before his majesty, and his hair measured, and found to be twelve cubits in length. The king then ordered food to be set before him, and after he was refreshed the betrothal ceremony was performed.

As it was now late they prevailed upon him to pass the night as the guest of the king. Early in the morning he set out, but, as he had a long distance to go, the day was far advanced before he reached the place where his cattle were. They were angry at having been kept penned up to so late an hour, and as he removed the bars to let them out, they knocked him down, and trampled upon his hair in such a way, as to pull it all out leaving him bald. Not being daunted, he collected his cows, and started on his return journey, but us he drove them along, one after another they vanished, so that only a few remained when he reached the king's palace.

There were two brothers named Kara and Guja. Guja, who was the elder, did the work at home, and Kara was a ploughman. One day the two went to the forest to dig edible roots.

On his arrival they noticed that he had lost all his hair, and on being questioned he related to the king all that had fallen upon him. His hair being gone the princess refused to marry him, so instead of becoming the king's son-in-law, he became one of his hired servants.

The Story of Kara and Guja

There were two brothers named Kara and Guja. Guja, who was the elder, did the work at home, and Kara was a ploughman. One day the two went to the forest to dig edible roots. After they had been thus engaged for some hours, Kara said to Guja, "Look up and see the sun's position in the heavens." Looking up he said, "Oh brother, one is rising and another is setting." They then said, "The day is not yet past, let us stir ourselves, and lose no time." So they dug with all their might.

After digging a long time, Kara looked up and became aware that it was night. He then exclaimed, "Oh brother, it is now night, what shall we do? Come let us seek some place where we can remain until the morning." After they had wandered awhile in the forest they spied a light in the distance, and on drawing near they found that a tiger had kindled a fire, and was warming himself. Going up to the entrance to the cave they called out to the tiger, "Oh uncle, give us a place to sleep in." He answered, "Come in." So the two went in, and being hungry began to roast and eat the roots they had brought with them. The tiger hearing them eating, enquired what it was. They replied, "Oh uncle, we are roasting and eating the roots which we dug up in the forest." He then said, "Oh my nephews, I will also try how they taste." So they handed him a piece of charcoal, and as he munched it he said, "Oh my nephews, how is it that I feel it grating between my teeth?" They replied, "It is an old one that you have got, uncle." He then said,"Give me another, and I will try it." So they gave him another piece of charcoal, and after he had crunched it awhile he said, "Oh my nephews, this is as bad as the other," to which they rejoined, "Oh uncle,your mouth is old, therefore what is good to us, is the reverse to you." The tiger did not wish to try his grinders on another piece of charcoal, so the brothers were left to enjoy their repast alone.

The tiger after losing his tail summoned a council of all the tigers inhabiting that part of the forest, at which they decided to kill and eat the two brothers.

After they had eaten all the roots, Guja said to Kara, "What shall we eat now? Come let us eat this old tiger's tail." Kara replied,"Do not talk in that way, brother, the tiger will devour us." "Not so, brother," said Guja, "I have a great desire to eat flesh." The old tiger understood their conversation, and being afraid tried to get out of the cave, but the brothers caught hold of him, and wrenched off his tail, which they roasted in the ashes, and then ate.

The tiger after losing his tail summoned a council of all the tigers inhabiting that part of the forest, at which they decided to kill and eat the two brothers. So they went to the cave, but Kara and Guja had fled, and had taken refuge in a palm tree which grew on the edge of a large deep tank. Not finding them in the cave the tigers, headed by him who had lost his tail, went in quest of them, and coming to the tank saw them reflected in the water, and one after another they dived in, thinking they would be able to seize them, but of course they could not catch a shadow. One of the tigers, when in the act of yawning, looked upwards, and seeing them in the tree exclaimed, "There they are. There they are." They then asked the brothers how they had managed to climb up, to which they replied, "We stood one ach other's shoulders." The tigers then said, "Come, let us do the same, and we shall soon reach them." As the tail-less tiger was most interested in their capture, they made him stand lowest, and a tiger climbed up and stood on his shoulders, and another on his, and soon; but before they reached the brothers, Kara called out to Guja, "Give me your sharp battle-axe, and I shall hamstring the tail-less tiger." The tail-less tiger forgetting himself jumped to one side, and the whole pillar of tigers fell in a heap on the ground. They now began to abuse the old tail-less tiger, who fearing lest they should tear him in pieces fled into the forest.

After the tigers had left, the two brothers descended from the palm tree, and walked rapidly away as they dreaded that the tigers might yet follow them. Towards evening they came to a village, and entering into the house of an old woman lay down to sleep. The owner of the house observing them said, "Oh my children, do not sleep tonight, for there is a demon who visits in rotation each house in the village, and each time he comes carries off some one and eats him; it is my turn to receive a visit tonight." They said, "Do not trouble us now,let us sleep, as we are tired." So they slept, but kept their weather eye open. During the night the old woman came quietly, and began

> *About midnight the demon came, and as he was entering the house, Kara and Guja shot at him with their bows and arrows, and he fell down dead.*

to bite their arms, which they had laid aside before retiring to rest. Hearing a sound as if someone were crunching iron between his teeth, the brothers called out, "Old woman, what are you eating?" She replied "Only a few roasted peas which I brought from the chief's house." About midnight the demon came, and as he was entering the house, Kara and Guja shot at him with their bows and arrows, and he fell down dead. Then they cut out his claws and tongue, and placed them in a bag. Afterwards they threw out the body of the demon into the garden behind the house.

Now it so happened that the king had promised to give his daughter and half of his kingdom to the man who should slay the demon. Early in the morning a Dome, who was passing, discovered the body of the demon, and said within himself, "I will take it to the king and claim the reward." So running home he broke all the furniture in his house and beat his old woman saying, "Get out of this house. I am about to bring the king's daughter home as my bride." He then returned quickly, and taking up the body of the demon carried it to the king, and said, "Oh sir king, I have slain the demon." The king replied, "Very well, we will enquire into it." So he commanded some of his servants to examine the body, and on doing so they found that the claws had been extracted and the tongue cut out. They reported the condition of the body to the king, who ordered the Dome to state the weapon with which he killed him. The Dome replied, "I hit him with a club on the head." On the head being examined no mark whatever was seen, so in order to arrive at the truth the king ordered all the inhabitants of

The king sentenced the Dome to be beaten and driven from the village. After receiving his stripes, the Dome returned home, and gathered the shreds of his property together.

the village to be brought together to the palace. He then enquired of them as to who killed the demon.

The old woman, in whose house Kara and Guja had passed the night, stepped forward and said, "Oh sir king, two strangers came to my house yesterday evening, and during the night they slew the demon." The king said, "Where are those two men?" The old woman replied, "There they are, the two walking together." So the king sent and brought them back, and questioned them as to the slaying of the demon. They pointed out the arrow-marks on the body, and produced his claws and tongue from their bag. This evidence convinced the king that they, and not the Dome, had slain the demon. Kara and Guja were received with great favour by the king, and received the promised reward.

The king sentenced the Dome to be beaten and driven from the village. After receiving his stripes, the Dome returned home, and gathered the shreds of his property together. He also went in search of his Dome wife and children, but they mocked him saying, "You went to marry the king's daughter, why do you come again seeking us."

Thus Kara and Guja gained a kingdom.

The King and his Inquisitive Queen

There was a certain king known by the name of Huntsman, on account of his expertness in the chase. One day when returning from the forest where he had been hunting he found a serpent and a lizard fighting on the path along which he was moving. As they were blocking the way he ordered them to stand aside and allow him to pass, but they gave no heed to what he said. King Huntsman then began to beat them with his staff. He killed the lizard, but the serpent fled, and so escaped.

The serpent then went to Monsha, the king of the serpents, and complained of the treatment the lizard and himself had received at the hands of King Huntsman. The next day king Monsha went and met King Huntsman on his way home from the forest, and blocked his way so that he could not pass. King Huntsman being angry said, "Clear the way, and allow me to pass, or else I shall send an arrow into you. Why do you block my way?" King Monsha replied, "Why did you assault the lizard and the serpent, with intent to kill them both?" King Huntsman answered, "I ordered them to get out of my way, but they would not, I therefore assaulted them, and killed one. The other saved himself by flight." King Monsha

The serpent then went to Monsha, the king of the serpents, and complained of the treatment the lizard and himself had received at the hands of King Huntsman.

hearing this explanation said, "Very good, the fault was theirs, not yours."

King Huntsman then petitioned the king of the serpents to bestow upon him the gift of understanding the language of animals and insects. King Monsha acceded to his request, and gave him the gift he desired.

A few days after this event King Huntsman went to the forest, and after hunting all day returned home in the evening. Having washed his hands and feet, he sat down to his meal of boiled rice. When the rice was being served to the king a few grains fell on the ground, and a fly and an ant began to dispute as to who should carry them away. The fly said, "I will take them to my children." The ant replied, "No, I will take them to mine." Hearing the two talk, the king was amused, and began to smile. The queen, who was standing by, said to him, "Tell me what has made you laugh." On being thus addressed the king became greatly confused, for at the time the gift of understanding the language of animals and insects was bestowed upon him, King Monsha had forbidden him to make it known to anyone. He had said, "If you tell this to any one, I shall eat you." Remembering this, the king feared to answer the question put to him by the queen. He tried to deceive her by saying, "I did not laugh, you must have been mistaken." She would not, however, be thus put off, so the king was obliged to tell her that if he answered her question his life would be forfeited. The queen was inexorable, and said, "Whether you forfeit your life or not, you must tell me." The king then said,

"Well, if it must be so, let us make ready to go to the bank of the Ganges. There I shall tell you, and when I have done so you must push me into the river, and then return home."

Do not think to make me like this foolish king, who vainly tries to please a woman. He has come here to lose his own life at the bidding of one. You tell me to go and bring you grass out of such a flood as this.

The king armed himself, and the two set out for the river. When they had reached it, they sat down to rest under the shade of a tree. A flock of goats was grazing near to where they were seated, and the king's attention was arrested by a conversation which was being carried on between an old she-goat and a young he-goat. The former addressed the latter thus, "There is an island in the middle of the Ganges, and on that island there is a large quantity of good sweet grass. Get the grass for me, and I shall give you my daughter in marriage." The he-goat was not thus to be imposed upon. He angrily addressed his female friend as follows, "Do not think to make me like this foolish king, who vainly tries to please a woman. He has come here to lose his own life at the bidding of one. You tell me to go and bring you grass out of such a flood as this. I am no such fool. I do not care to die yet. There are many more girls quite as good as your daughter."

The king understood what passed between them, and admitted to himself the truth of what the he-goat had said. After considering a short time he arose, and having made long a rude sacrificial altar, he said to the queen, "Kneel down, and do me obeisance, and I shall tell you what made me laugh." She knelt down, and the king struck off her head and burnt her body upon the altar. Returning home he performed her funeral ceremonies, after which he married another wife.

He reigned prosperously for many years, and decided all disputes that were brought before him by animals or insects.

The Story of Bitaram

In a certain village there lived seven brothers. The youngest of them planted a certain vegetable, and went every day to examine it to see how it was growing. For a long time there were only the stalk and leaves, but at length a flower appeared, and from it a fruit. This fruit he measured daily to mark its growth. It grew continuously until it became exactly a span long, after which it remained stationary. One day he said to his sisters-in-law, "Do not eat my fruit, for whoever does so will give birth to a child only one span long." He continued his daily visits to his plant as usual, and was pleased to note that the fruit was evidently ripening. One day, during his absence, one of his sisters-in-law plucked the fruit and ate it. On returning from the field where he had been ploughing, he went to look at and measure his fruit, but it was gone, it had been stolen. Suspecting that one of his sisters-in-law was the thief, he accused each of them in turn, but they all denied having touched it. When he found that no one would confess to having taken it, he said to them, "Do not tell upon yourselves, the thief will be caught before long." And so it happened, for one of them gave birth to a baby of one span length. The first time he saw his sister-in-law after the child was born he laughed, and said to her, "You denied having stolen my fruit, now you see I have found you out."

One day he surprised his mother by saying, "Let me take the food to my father and uncles today." She replied, "What a fancy! You, child, are only a span high, how can you carry it?"

When the time came that the child should receive a name, Bitaram was given to him, because he was only a span in height. Bitaram's mother used to take food to the brothers to the field when they were ploughing, and when Bitaram was able to walk so far he accompanied her. One day he surprised his mother by saying, "Let me take the food to my father and uncles today." She replied, "What a fancy! You, child, are only a span high, how can you carry it?" But Bitaram insisted saying, "I can carry it well enough, and carry it I will." His mother being unable to resist his pertinacity said, "Then, child, take it, and be off." So she placed the basket on his head and he set out. Arrived at the field he went up a furrow,

When the cattle returned without Bitaram, his father and uncles became alarmed for his safety, and immediately went in search of him. They went here and there calling out, "Bitaram, where are you?"

but the ground was so uneven that before he reached his destination, he had lost nearly all the rice, which had been shaken out of the basket. On his coming near, one of his uncles called out, "Is that you Bitaram?" He replied, "Yes, it is I, Bitaram." Climbing up out of the furrow, he put down the basket saying, "Help yourselves, and I will take the oxen and buffaloes to the water." So saying, he drove off the cattle to the river. When they had quenched their thirst, he gathered them together and began to drive them back again to where he had left his father and uncles. While following them up the sandy back of the river, he fell into a depression made by the hoof of a buffalo, and was soon covered up by the loose sand sent rolling down by the herd as they ascended.

When the cattle returned without Bitaram, his father and uncles became alarmed for his safety, and immediately went in search of him. They went here and there calling out, "Bitaram, where are you?" But failing to find him they concluded that he had been devoured by some wild animal, and returned sorrowfully home. Rain fell during the night,and washed the sand from off

Bitaram, so that he was able to get up, and climb out. On his way home he encountered some thieves who were dividing their booty in a lonely part of the forest. Bitaram hearing them disputing called out, "Kehe kere" at the pitch of his voice. The thieves hearing the sound, looked round on all sides to see who was near, but the night being dark, and they not directing their eyes near enough to the ground to see Bitaram, they could discern no one. Then they said to each other, "Let us seek safety in flight. A spirit has been sent to watch us." So they all made off leaving behind them the brass vessels they had stolen. Bitaram gathered these up, and hid them among some prickly bushes, and then went home.

It was now past midnight, and all had retired to rest, and as Bitaram stood shivering with cold at the closed door, he called out, "Open the door and let me in." His father hearing him said, "Is that you Bitaram?" He replied, "Yes, open the door." They then enquired where he had been, and he related all that had happened to him after he had driven the cattle to the river. Having warmed himself at the fire, he told his father of his adventure with the thieves in the forest. He said, "I despoiled some thieves, whom I met in the jungle, of the brass vessels they had stolen." His father replied, "Foolish child, do not tell lies, you yourself are not the height of a brass lota (drinking-cup)." "No father," said Bitaram, "I am telling the truth, come and I will show you where they are." His father and uncles went with him, and he pointed out to them the vessels hidden among the prickly bushes. They

Early next morning some sepoys, who were searching for the thieves, happened to pass that way, and seeing the stolen property lying outside of the house, recognized it, and apprehended Bitaram's father and uncles and dragged them off to prison.

picked them all up and brought them home.

Early next morning some sepoys, who were searching for the thieves, happened to pass that way, and seeing the stolen property lying outside of the house, recognized it, and apprehended Bitaram's father and uncles and dragged them off to prison. After this Bitaram and his mother were obliged to beg their bread from house to house. She often attributed him to the misery which had befallen them, saying, "Had it not been for your pertinacity, your father and uncles would not have been deprived of their liberty."

One day, as they were following their usual avocation, they entered a certain house, and Bitaram said to his mother, "Ask the people of the house to give me a tumki." She did not at first comply, but he kept urging her until being irritated she said, "It was through your pertinacity in insisting upon being allowed to carry the food to your father and uncles that they are now bound and in prison, and yet you will not give up the bad habit." Bitaram said, "No, mother, do ask it for me." As he would not be silenced she begged it for him, and the people kindly gave it.

Bitaram then strapped the bag of flour on the cat's back as a saddle, and mounted. Puss, however, refused to go in the direction desired, and it was with great difficulty that he prevailed upon her to take the road.

At the next house they came to, they saw a cat walking about, and Bitaram said, "Oh mother, ask the people to give me the cat." As before, she at first refused, but he continued to press her, and she becoming annoyed scolded him saying, "The young gentleman insists on obtaining this and that. It was your pertinacity that caused your father and uncles to be dragged to prison in bonds." Bitaram replied, "Not so, mother, do ask them to give me the cat." As the only way to silence him she said to the people of the house, "Give my boy your cat, he will hold it in his arms for a few minutes, and then set it down". But he carried it away with him. Bitaram then begged his mother to make him a bag, and fill it with flour, saying, "I am going to obtain the release of my father and uncles." She mockingly replied, "Much you can do." She made him a bag, however, and filling it with flour said,"Be off."

Bitaram then strapped the bag of flour on the cat's back as a saddle, and mounted. Puss, however, refused to go in the direction desired, and it was with great difficulty that he prevailed upon her to take the road. As he rode along he observed a swarm of bees on an an thill, and dismounting he addressed them as follows, "Come bees, go in, come bees, go in." The bees swarmed into the tumki, and Bitaram having covered them up with a leaf continued his journey. Before he had gone far he came to a large tank, which belonged to the raja who had imprisoned his father. A number of women had come to the tank for water, and Bitaram taking his stand upon the embankment began to shoot arrows at their water pots. After he had broken several, the women spied him mounted on his cat with his bow and arrows in his hand,and believing him to be an elf from the forest fled in terror to the city. Going to the raja they said "Oh raja, come and see. Someone is on the tank embankment. We do not know who or what he is, but he is only a span high." The raja then summoned his soldiers, and commanded them to take their bows and arrows, and go and shoot him whoever he was. The soldiers went within range, but although they shot away all their arrows, they failed to hit him. So returning to the raja they said, "He cannot be shot." Hearing this, raja became angry, and calling for his bow and arrows, went to the tank and began to shoot at Bitaram, but although he persevered until his right side ached with drawing the bow, he could not hit him.

When he desisted, Bitaram called out, "Are you exhausted?" The raja answered, "Yes." Then said Bitaram, "It is my turn now," and taking the leaf off from the mouth of the basket called to the bees, "Go into the battle, bees." The bees issued from the basket like a black rope, and tung the raja and those who were with him. No way of escape offering, the raja called out to Bitaram, "Call off your bees, and I will give you the half of my kingdom and my daughter, and I will also set at liberty your father and uncles." Bitaram gathered the bees into thebasket, and after his father and uncles had been released, took them back to the ant hill from whence he had brought them. On his return he wedded the princess and received half of her father's kingdom.

Bitaram and his wife lived happily together, and every thing they took in hand prospered, so before long they were richer than the king himself.

Bitaram and his wife lived happily together, and every thing they took in hand prospered, so before long they were richer than the king himself. One great source of Bitaram's wealth was a cow which the princess had brought him as part of her dowry. Being envious of their good fortune, the raja and his sons resolved to kill the cow and thus obtain possession of all the gold and silver. So they put the cow to death, but when they had cut her up they were disappointed as neither gold nor silver were found in her stomach.

Bitaram placed his cow's hide in the sun, and when it was dry, carried it away to sell it. Darkness coming on he climbed into a tree for safety, as wild beasts infested the forest through which he was passing. During the night some thieves came under the tree in which he was, and began to divide the money they had stolen. Bitaram then

They were ashamed and angry at having allowed themselves to be thus imposed upon by Bitaram, and in revenge they set fire to his house at night, but he crept into a rat's hole and so escaped injury.

relaxed his hold of the dry hide, which made such a noise as it fell from branch to branch that the thieves fled terror-stricken, and left all their booty behind them. In the morning Bitaram descended, and collecting all the rupees carried them home. He then showed the money to his wife, and said "Go and ask to loan of your father's paila, so that I may measure them." So she went and brought the measure, which had several cracks in it. Having measured his money he sent back the raja's paila, but he had not noticed that one or two pieces were left sticking in the cracks. So they said to him, "Where did you get the money?" He replied "By the sale of my cow's hide." Hearing this they said, "Will the merchant who bought yours, buy any more?" He said, "Yes. I received all this money for my one hide, how much more may not you receive seeing you have such large herds of cattle! If you dispose of their hides at the same rate as I have done, you will secure immense wealth." So they killed all their cattle, but when they offered the hides for sale they found they had been hoaxed. They were ashamed and angry at having allowed themselves to be thus imposed upon by Bitaram, and in revenge they set fire to his house at night, but he crept into a rat's hole and so escaped injury. In the morning he emerged from his hiding place, and carefully gathering up the ashes of his house tied them up in a cloth, and carried them away. As he walked along he met a merchant, to whom he said, "What you have in your bag?" He replied "Gold-pieces only." The merchant then enquired of Bitaram what he had tied up in his cloth, to which he answered, "Gold-dust only." Bitaram then said, "Will you exchange?" The merchant said, "Yes." So they exchanged,and Bitaram returned laden with gold. Not being able to count it, he again sent his wife to borrow her father's paila, and having measured the gold-pieces returned it to him. This time a few pieces of gold remained in the cracks in the paila, and the raja, being informed of it, went and asked Bitaram where he got the gold. He replied, "I sold the ashes of my house which you burnt over my head, and received the gold in return." The raja and his sons then enquired if the merchant,who bought the ashes from him, would buy any more. Bitaram replied, "Yes, he will buy all he can get." "Do you think," said they, "he will buy from us?" Bitaram advised them to burn their houses, and like him, turn the ashes into gold. "I had only one small house," he said, "and I obtained all this money. You have larger houses, and should therefore receive a correspondingly large amount." So they set fire to, and burnt their houses, and gathering up the ashes took them to the bazar, and there offered them for sale. After they had gone the whole length of the bazar, and had met with no buyers, someone advised them to go to where the washermen lived, saying, they might possibly take

Bitaram on escaping collected all the herd boy's cattle, and drove them home. When the raja and his sons returned, they found Bitaram with a large herd of cows and buffaloes. Going near, they enquired where he had got them.

them. The washermen, however, refused, and as they could not find a purchaser, they threw away the ashes, and returned home determined to take revenge upon Bitaram.

This time they decided upon drowning him, so one day they seized him, and putting him into a bag they carried him to the river. Arriving there, they put him down, and went to some little distance to cook their food. In the meantime a herd boy came up and asked Bitaram why he was tied up in the bag. He replied, "They are taking me away to marry me against my will." The herd boy said, "I will go instead of you. I wish to be married." Bitaram replied, "Open the bag and let me out, and you get in, and I will tie it up again." So Bitaram was released, and the herd boy took his place, and was afterwards thrown into the river and he drowned.

Bitaram on escaping collected all the herd boy's cattle, and drove them home. When the raja and his sons returned, they found Bitaram with a large herd of cows and buffaloes. Going near, they enquired where he had got them. He replied, "At some distance below the spot where you threw me into the river, I found numerous herds of cattle, so I brought away as many as one person could drive. If you all go, you will be able to bring a very much larger number." So they said, "Very well, put us into bags, and tie us up as we did to you." Bitaram replied, "It is impossible for me to carry you as you did to me. Walk to the river bank, and there get into the bags, and I will push you into the river." They did as he suggested, and when all was in readiness, he pushed them into the river, and they were all drowned.

One day, very suddenly, the hen-sparrow took ill, and died. The next day the cock-sparrow appeared with another mate, and sat in front of the nest with her, as he had done with the other.

Bitaram returned alone, and took possession of all that had belonged to them. The whole kingdom became his, and he reigned peacefully as long as he lived.

The Story of Sit and Bosont

There was a certain raja that had two sons named Sit and Bosont. Their mother the rani had been long ill, and the raja was greatly dejected on her account. From the bed on which she lay, the rani could see two sparrows that had made their nest in a hole in the wall of the palace, and she had remarked the great love and tenderness which the hen-sparrow bore towards her young ones. One day she saw both sparrows sitting in front of their nest. The sight of them set her thinking, and she came to the conclusion that the hen-sparrow was a model mother. The raja also had his attention attracted daily by the sparrows. One day, very suddenly, the hen-sparrow took ill, and died. The next day the cock-sparrow appeared with another mate, and sat in front of the nest with her, as he had done with the other. But the new mother took no notice of the young ones in the nest, but left them to die of hunger. The rani, who was greatly grieved to see such want of compassion, said to the raja, "This is how it is, one has no pity for those who belong to another. Remember what you have been a witness of, and should I die take care of the two children." Shortly after this the rani died, and the raja mourned over her, and continued most solicitous for the welfare of their two boys.

Some months after the rani's death, the raja's subjects prayed him to take another wife, saying, "Without a rani your kingdom is incomplete." The raja refused to comply, saying, "I shall never take another wife." His subjects would not, however, be silenced, but continued to press the matter upon him with such persistency that eventually he had to accede to their wishes, and take to himself another partner. He continued, however, to love and cherish his two sons Sit and Bosont.

Sometime after their marriage the rani took a dislike to the elder son Sit, and was determined that he should no longer be allowed to remain within the precincts of the palace. So she feigned sickness, and the raja summoned physicians from all parts of his dominions, but without avail, as none of them could tell what the disease was from which the rani was suffering. One day when Sit and Bosont were out of the way, and the raja and she were alone together, she said to him, "Doctors and medicines will not save my life, but if you will listen to me, and do what I tell you, I shall completely recover." The raja said, "Let me hear what it is, and I shall try what effect it may have." The rani said, "If you will promise to do for me what I shall request, I will tell you, and not otherwise." The raja replied, "I shall certainly comply with your wishes." The rani again said, "Will you without doubt, do what I wish?" The raja replied, "Yes, I shall." After she had made him promise a third time she said, "Will you take oath that you will not seek to evade fulfilling my desire?" The raja said, "I take my oath that I shall carry out your wishes to the full extent of my ability." Having thus prevailed upon the raja to pledge his word of honour, she said, "Do not allow your eldest son, Sit, to remain any longer in the palace. Order him to leave, and go somewhere else, so that I may not see his face, and never to return."

In his anxiety to save the life of his rani, he had bound himself by an oath before he knew what it was he would be required to do.

On hearing this raja was greatly distressed. But what could he do? The rani had said, "If you permit him to remain, I shall die, and if you fulfil my wishes I shall live," and in his anxiety to save the life of his rani, he had bound himself by an oath before he knew what it was he would be required to do. After much consideration as to how he could

On hearing his brother'swords, Bosont's heart was filled with sorrow, and he replied, "Not so, I cannot see you go away alone. You have been guilty of no fault for which our parents could send you away.

best communicate the order to leave the palace to his son, he decided to write it on a sheet of paper and fix it, during his absence, to the door of his room. When the brothers returned, they found the paper placed there by the raja, and on reading it, were greatly troubled. After some time, during which Sit had been considering the position in which he found himself, he said to his brother, "You must remain, and I must go." On hearing his brother's words, Bosont's heart was filled with sorrow, and he replied, "Not so, I cannot see you go away alone. You have been guilty of no fault for which our parents could send you away. I cannot remain here alone. I will accompany you. We are children of the same mother, and we should not part." His brother replied, "Let us leave the house today. We can pass the night in some place close at hand." So they left their father's house, and concealed themselves in its vicinity. On the approach of evening they began to feel the pangs of hunger, and the younger said to the elder, "What shall we do? We have no food." After a minute's thought, the elder replied, "Although we have been sent adrift, we will take our elephants, and horses, and clothes, and money along with us." So when night had fallen, they entered the palace and brought out all that belonged to them, and at cock-crow, set forth on their journey. They travelled all day, and as the sun began to decline, they reached a dense jungle, and passing through it they came to a large city where they put up for the night. The city pleased them much, and they hired quarters in the Sarai. After they had gained a little acquaintance with their surroundings, Sit, attired in gorgeous apparel, and mounted on a splendid horse, rode every evening through the principal streets of the city. One evening the daughter of the raja of that country, from the roof of the palace, saw him ride past, and fell deeply in love with him. She immediately descended to her room, and feigning sickness, threw herself upon her couch. Her parents, on entering, found her weeping bitterly,and on enquiring the cause were informed by her attendants that she had been suddenly seized with a dangerous illness, the nature of which they did not know. The raja at once summoned the most famed physicians that could be found, to cure his daughter. One after another, however, failed to understand her complaint, and she grew worse daily. She was heard continually wailing, "I shall never recover; I shall die." After the doctors had retired baffled, she

One evening the daughter of the raja of that country, from the roof of the palace, saw him ride past, and fell deeply in love with him.

"Of late we have daily seen a young man in dazzling white apparel, riding and curveting his horse through the city; if you betroth me to that young prince, I shall enjoy my accustomed health again."

addressed her parents as follows; "You, who gave me life, listen to my entreaty. There is one expedient still, which if you will agree to put into execution, I shall recover, and be as well as formerly, and should you refuse to do as I say, and call it foolishness, then you shall never see my face again, I shall depart this life at once." On hearing these words, her parents said, "Tell us, what it is, we will surely act agreeably to your wishes." She replied, "Oh! Father, promise me that you will carry them out without reserve." Her parents then promised with an oath, that they would do all she desired. Then she told her story, "Of late we have daily seen a young man in dazzling white apparel, riding and curveting his horse through the city; if you betroth me to that young prince, I shall enjoy my accustomed health again."

On hearing this, her parents became greatly distressed, as they were averse to betrothing their daughter to a stranger of whom they knew nothing. After consulting together they said, "He comes this way in the evening, let us look out for him, and see what he is like." About sunset, Sit, mounted on his horse, rode in the direction of the palace. The raja had given orders to some of his attendants to arrest the man who, every evening dressed in white, rode past the palace. So, on his appearing, they laid hold of him and led him into the presence of the raja, who being pleased with his appearance, at once introduced him to his daughter's room. She, on beholding him, instantly became well, and that same evening the two were married.

Bosont having charge of the property remained in the Sarai, while his brother went out riding. Sit not returning at his usual time, Bosont was alarmed and waited anxiously for his return. At length, being wearied, he fell asleep. During the night a gang of thieves entered his room, and began to carry off all his valuables. Bosont slept so soundly that they had time to take away everything save his bed and clothes. To obtain possession of these they had to lift him, onwhich he awoke and gave the alarm. The thieves beat him with their clubs till he was half dead; then, senseless and with a broken leg, they threw him into the dry bed of a river.

In the morning his servants became aware of the robbery, and also that their master was missing. His servants found him sometime after in the river bed, and carried him to a doctor who bound up his limb, and took care of him. He was soon well enough to move about, but doomed to limp through life.

Whenever a ship left the port on its outward voyage, it was customary to carry a man on board, who, on the rising of a storm at sea, was cast over board to appease to wrath of the Spirit of the mighty Deep.

The raja of that country was very wealthy, and had ships on the sea. Whenever a ship left the port on its outward voyage, it was customary to carry a man on board, who, on the rising of a storm at sea, was cast over board to appease to wrath of the Spirit of the mighty Deep. Without such a victim on board, no ship could leave the harbour. Now, it so happened that one of the raja's vessels was about to sail to a foreign port, but no man suitable for the sacrifice could be obtained. At last the raja ordered them to take the lame man, whom he had seen limping about the city. He, not knowing the purpose they had in view in asking him to accompany them on their voyage, gladly embraced the opportunity of seeing foreign lands. No sooner was he on board than the ship began to move, and to obtain a better view he climbed up the mast, and sat on the top of it. In twelve days they reached a port. Bosont, however, did not descend from his elevated station, but continued gazing on the country lying around.

The daughter of the raja of that city, while walking on the roof of the palace, enjoying the cool of the evening, saw Bosont seated on the ship's mast. She at once fell violently in love with him, and descending to her room, feigned sickness. Her parents called in the most famed physicians, but their skill was of no avail, the young lady's illness increased in intensity. At last, when her parents began to give up hope of saving her life, she said, "The doctors cannot do me any good, but if you will do as I direct you, I shall recover." They said, "Tell us what it is that we can do for you." She replied, "Before I can make it known to you, you must take oath that you will not seek to evade the performance of it." To this they agreed, and the princess said, "If you will betroth me to the man

The Story of a Tiger

A certain man had charge of a number of cattle. One day he took them to graze near a quagmire, and leaving them there went in search of jungle fruits. It so happened that one of the bullocks was browsing on the edge of the quagmire when a tiger came creeping stealthily up, and sprang upon it, but somehow or other missed his mark, and fell into the quagmire and there stuck fast. When the herd come to drive his cattle home, he found the tiger fast in the mud, and called a large number of people to come and see him. The tiger addressed those who came to gaze upon him as follows, "Oh men, pull me out. I am in great straits." They replied, "We will not pull you out even to save your life. You are a ravenous animal." The tiger said, "I will not eat you." So they pulled him out. When he was again on dry land, he said, "I will devour you, for it is my nature to do so." They replied, "Will you really eat us?"

"Yes, I will," said the tiger. "Well", they rejoined, "if you will devour us, what can we do

But let us first ask the opinion of some others as to whether it is right for you to eat us or not." So they requested the opinion of all the trees in the forest, and each said, "Human beings are all bad."

to prevent you? But let us first ask the opinion of some others as to whether it is right for you to eat us or not." So they requested the opinion of all the trees in the forest, and each said, "Human beings are all bad." On asking the Mohwa tree, it replied, "Men are not good. Behold every year I give them my flowers to eat, and my fruit from which to make oil. In the hot weather I give them shade, and on leaving,when they have rested, they give me a parting slash with their axes, therefore it is right to eat these people, as they return evil for good." So said all the trees.

From this forest they went to another in which they found a cow to whom they said, "We are come to ask your opinion on a certain matter about which we are at variance. This tiger was up to the neck in a quagmire,and we pulled him out. Now he wishes to return evil for good. Is it right for him to do so?" The cow replied, "Yes, yes, I have heard what you have got to say. You human beings are not the correct thing. Behold me, how much I have contributed to the health and comfort of my master, yet he does not recognize my merit. Now that I am old, he has turned me out, and should I improve a little in condition, he will say, 'I will take this cow to the market and sell it. I will at least get a few pence for it.' Behold, when a man is well to do, he has many friends, but when he is poor, no one knows him. Verily, you are worthy to be devoured." The tiger then said to the men, "Well, have you heard all this? Are you convinced?" They said, "Hold on, let us ask one person more." So as they walked along they saw a jackal and called to him, "Oh uncle, stand still." The jackal said, "No I cannot wait, my companions, who are on their way to see the swinging festival, are far ahead of me, and I am hurrying to overtake them." They said to him, "Wait a little and settle this matter for us. We pulled this tiger out of a quagmire, and now he wishes to devour us." The jackal then said to the tiger, "Is this true? I cannot believe that a famed individual like yourself would be fool enough to jump into a quagmire. Come, show me the place, and how it happened." So the tiger led him to the quagmire, and said, "This is the place from which I sprang, and this is how I did it,"and he leaped into the quagmire. The jackal turning to the men, said, "What are you staring at? Pelt him with stones." So they all set to and stoned the tiger to death.

The jackal then said to the tiger, "Is this true? I cannot believe that a famed individual like yourself would be fool enough to jump into a quagmire.

Story of a Lizard, a Tiger, and a Lame Man

Once upon a time in a certain jungle, a lizard and a tiger were fighting, and a lame man, who was tending goats nearby, saw them. The tiger being beaten by the lizard was ashamed to own it, and coming to the lame man said, "Tell me which of us won." The lame man being in great fear lest the tiger should eat him, said, "You won." On another occasion the lizard was compelled to flee, and took refuge

So one day after an ignominious flight on the part of the tiger, he being, as usual, requested to give his opinion as to who won, said, "The lizard had the best of it." On hearing this, the tiger became angry.

in an ant hill. The tiger pursued him, but not being able to get him out, sat down to watch.

The lizard seeing his opportunity, crept stealthily up to his inveterate enemy, and climbing up his tail, fixed his teeth into his haunch, and held firmly on. The tiger felt the pain of the lizard's bite, but could not reach him to knock him off, so he ran to the lame man, and said, "Release me from this lizard." When he had caused the lizard to let go his grip, the tiger said, "Oh lame man, which of us won in the encounter?" The poor man in great fear said, "You won." The same scene was enacted daily for many days. The tiger always came to the lame man and said, "Knock off this lizard," and after he had done so, would say, "Which of us won?" The lame man invariably replied, "You won." This had happened so often that the lame man began to feel annoyed at having to tell a lie every day to please the tiger. So one day after an ignominious flight on the part of the tiger, he being, as usual, requested to give his opinion as to who won, said, "The lizard had the best of it." On hearing this, the tiger became angry,and said, "I shall eat you, my fine fellow, because you say the lizard defeated me. Tell me where you sleep." The poor lame man on hearing the tiger threaten him, thus, trembled with fear, and was silent. But the tiger pressed him. He said, "Tell at once, for I shall certainly devour you." The lame man replied, "I sleep in the wall press." When night fell, the tiger set off to eat the lame man, but after searching in the wall press failed to find him. In the morning the lame man led his goats out to graze, and again met the tiger, who addressed him as follows, "You are a great cheat. I did not find you in the wall press last night." The lame man replied, "How is it you did not find me? I was sleeping there." "No," said the tiger, "you were not, you have deceived me. Now, tell me truly where you sleep." "I sleep on a rafter," said the lame man. About midnight the tiger went again in search of him to eat him, but did not find him on the rafter, so he returned home. In the morning the lame man as usual led his goats out to graze, and again encountered the tiger, who said to him, "How now! Where do you sleep? I could not find you last night." The lame man rejoined, "That is strange, I was there all the same." The tiger said, "You are a consummate liar. Now tell me plainly where you sleep at night, for I shall without doubt eat you." The lame man replied, "I sleep in the fire-place." Again the tiger went at night, but could not find him. Next morning he met the lame man, and said to him, "No more tricks, tell me where you sleep." He, thrown off his guard, said, "In the gongo." The tiger then withdrew to his den to wait till night came on, and the lame man, cursing his indiscretion, with a heavy heart, drove his goats

The tiger being terrified at the prospect of again meeting his mortal enemy, the redoubtable lizard, threw down the gongo and fled, calling out, "I will not eat you. You have got the lizard with you."

homewards. Having made his charge safe for the night, he sat down feeling very miserable. He refused the food that was set before him,and continued bewailing his hard lot. In the hope of inducing him to eat, they gave him some mohwa wrapped in a sal leaf. This also failed to tempt him to eat; but he carried it with him when he crept into thegongo to sleep. At night the tiger came and lifting up the gongo felt it heavy, and said, "Well, are you inside?" He replied, "Yes, I am." So the tiger carried off the gongo with the lame man in it. By the time the tiger had gone a considerable distance, the lame man became hungry and said within himself, "I shall have to die in the end, but in the meantime I will appease my hunger." So he opened his small parcel of mohwa, and the dry leaf crackled as he did so. The noise frightened the tiger and he said, "What is it you are opening?" The lame man replied, "It is yesterday's lizard." "Hold! Hold!" exclaimed the tiger, "Do not let him out yet, let me get clear away first." The lame man said, "Not so, I will not wait, but will let him out at once." The tiger being terrified at the prospect of again meeting his mortal enemy, the redoubtable lizard, threw down the gongo and fled, calling out, "I will not eat you. You have got the lizard with you."

In this way the lame man by means of the lizard saved his life.

Handicrafts

Jadupatia painting is the most prominent handicraft of the Sautars. It is made on vertical scrolls of paper. Previously, the paintings were made on cloth scrolls. The scrolls are glued or sewn together and a piece of old cloth or calico are sewn to the end of the scroll to protect the paper from damaging.

The two ends of the cloth are sewn round pieces of bamboo, one of which acted as a roller around which the scroll could be wound. Finally a string is attached to one end to secure the wound-up scroll.

Sautar dancing poses or movements, leaping drummer or galloping horses are the common figures drawn. Vertical and horizontal lines are given more emphasis in the painting

with intervals of zigzag patterns. The animals depicted in the paintings are coloured in various

bright shades. Tigers are colored bright yellow, brown, grey or even blue or green. Their heads are extra large; teeth, claws and tongues are magnified and touches of red contribute to an image of terrifying force and danger. Elephants are coloured in blue and horses in red symbolizing an air of wealth and opulence. Women who normally wear white are shown in flaming red and their chocolate complexions changed to white or yellow color. The figures in Jadupatia are illustrated in full-face.

Bunch of goat hair are tied on a small stick or porcupine quill to make brushes. Earlier the paintings were done with natural colors made from vegetable matter or minerals. By the 1940's colors were available in the bazaars. Soot was used for black, vermilion for red and mud from the riverbed for a rich reddish brown. Despite limited colors and materials, jadupatua scrolls in the Sautar Parganas portray great varieties of expressions and

treatment and on the other hand, there is a consistent adherence to certain basic assumptions.

All scrolls depicted figures in a single flat plane and showed a mild indifference to naturalism.

The stories are depicted in a series of simple clear-cut images in panels divided by horizontal bands. Simple diagrammatic forms depict trees, flowers or rocks. The figures are depicted usually in a standard corrugated line linking forehead, nose, lips and chin and eyes were vastly enlarged.

There are seven themes of the scroll paintings made by jadupatuas in the Sautar Parganas. They are :

- Life in Death's kingdom
- The story of the creation of the Sautars as preserved in Sautar tradition
- The Sautar festival of Bahajatras
- Mass meetings of the Sautars for dancing
- The personification of Sautar clans
- A tiger or leopard often with a human rider and
- Finally, the adventures of Krishna with the milkmaid.

Jadupatia painting is also a major source of income of the Sautar community. They earn their living by wandering from village to village showing scrolls and chanting the traditional tribal stories of creation, death and life in the underworld. The scrolls consist of twenty or more indivdual story panels arranged vertically, which are unrolled and rerolled as the story is sung.

Costumes and Ornaments

The Sautar costume has seen variations in different timelines. Both men and women wear head gear, upper and lower garment. Bordered sarees, not more than seven cubits in length are worn by the Sautar women. Half of this serves as the lower garments being knotted at the waist; the other is passed over the left shoulder and hangs in the front. No veils are used for their heads. The wavy bacl hair are combed and kept in a nice knob at the back of their head. Flowers and leaves are used to decorate them. Silk red ribbons are also used frequently. Under the age of five, the children wear very short loin cloth. Danda Jbinjbir is a coloured cloth tied at the waist. They also call it gendre. Panhand, a kind of sari is worn by the girls after they attain the age of ten years. Panhands are often designed with bright violet border.

Such saris reach only up to the knee as they measure three cubits in length and one and half cubits in wide. The upper part of their bodies are covered with another part of measurement called gamcha.

The women retain their primitive style of dressing making several pleats in the portion bound round the waist at the front and the end thrown over the shoulder from behind falls over the breast, and the edges are tucked in one either side into the portion round the middle.

Five cloths swen together, popularly known as Kantha are also worn by the women which are thrown over the shoulder to cover the breast.

Sautar men wear a short cloth tied at the waist. For free movement, the end of the cloth is passed on and secured near the end of the spine. Panchi is the loin cloth that the Sautars wear at home. They put on long sheet of thick cloth five cubits in width which they term kutcha.

Ornaments are worn by both male and female. The Sautar women use colourful flowers to decorate their hair, and over their ears but those who can afford use ornaments of various kinds, they wear ornaments made from nickel and silver. The average woman wears convex-shaped anklets (paina). They also use on their feet ornament call kharua and with a ring on her first finger of the toe. Their wrist has ornamented wristlets called phora sakom. They use several verities of rings like taka mudam, tunki mudam.

While some well to do Sautar wear a head ornament called jhipjhipi a silver tiara-like ornament, with a crescent moon glimmering a locket. Danda jhinjhir is decorated on the wrist. They decorate their ear lobs with jhinka. And the upper ears sparkle with khutla with five chains of silver swinging from it. Where as the necks have beautiful aids in the shape of hansulis. The materials used for preparing ornaments are brass, bronze, silver, nickel and gold.

❑

7

Challenges for Identity and Livelihood

The Sautars are originally nature worshippers and follow animism, i.e, they worship the supernatural power, plants, inanimate objects and natural phenomena. In initial days, the Sautars were deprived of their social status, rights and identity. As, the population suffered from poverty, it was being difficult for them to survive, let alone developing an identity. The Christians, taking advantage of their economic weakness and uneducation, started converting the Sautars to Christians with an advantage of very little benefit.

The non-tribal population or the Aryan community were very dominating. The Dev, Devtas of the Aryans were worshiped with gait and galore and they imbibed this religious practice into the weaker section of the society as well. The Sautars, hence, fell prey to the domination and started worshipping the Aryan God and Goddesses in place of nature. They began offering prayers to idols and adopted their religious practices.

It is alarming that the Sautar Christians or Hindus have niether developed proper knowledge about the philosophy of Christians or Hindus nor of the Sautar religion. They were persuaded towards conversation by the want or desire of proper recognition and social status. This did not help much as they still suffered from identity crisis.

In past days, the feudal lords ofetn engaged into fights with their oponents for land oriented matters. They used to hire the Sautars who were perfectly skilled in archery, to fight on their behalf. In return, they were paid very scantily. The Sautars, from both sides engaged into war and this resulted in the death of many innocent Sautars. Whereas, the feudal lords, between whom the fight was, remained safe. This unjust practice was quite prevelant in Bihar. As the Sautars were always hired to fight for the elite class, they were wrongly identified as criminal class of the society, whereas, they fought to earn a living. This belief is somehow, still exists in the society.

Sautars are agrarian community. They initially practiced Jhum cultivation (shifting agriculture). Being soulfully attached to the land and harvest, it was their right to be able to settle down and practice agriculture as their living. Yet, they were deprivedof landownership. The feudal lords/elites owned lands and the Sautars simply worked as agricultural labourers. Sautars also excelled in domination of animals but they only acquired the status of labours. Even after Independence, there was no law or policy established in favour of land owership to the Sautars. Also, they were deprived of education. Some of the people from the community, who are previledged wnough to recieve quality education, are preferring to move away from the Sautar traditional society and settle in other regions. Until and unless the education seeps into the community it becomes a challenge for them to prosper.

❑

8

Conclusion

Bihar, the land which homes 32 tribes, are enriched with the diversity of their culture, tradition, social and religious values. Among all other tribes, the Sautars are the most populous in Bihar. Their life is dependent on agriculture, forest trees and plants. The tribe are also engaged in fishing. They have acquired magnificent skill of making musical equipment, mats and baskets out is worth wathing. Sautar and nature are inseperable.

Sautars belong to the Proto-Australoid racial group and linguistically belong to the Mundari group of Austro-Asiatic linguistic family. Ol Chiki was developed by Dr Raghunath Murmu in the year 1925 as the Santhal script. It uses 30 letters and five basic diacritics. It has 6 basic vowels and three additional vowels, generated using the Gahla Tudag. The race is believed to belong to the ancient hunter-gatherer people who descended from the first major wave of anatomically modern humans to leave Africa around 50,000 years ago. They are characterised by gracile body types, they are thought to have had dark skin colour, approaching black, and wavy or curly black hair, low forehead, thick lips and wide jaw.

Histories of Sautars can also be traced from songs and folklore of the tribe. Historians from different region have come and wrote different things regarding them and large populations believe that is only the truth about Sautars. The primary occupation of the tribe is settled agriculture. Both men and women are engaged in this pursuit. Seasonal forest collectionis one of the important sources of subsidiary income. They collect minor forest produce like roots, fruits, tubers, green leaves, yams, honey, mahua flowers, etc. That sustains them for 3 to 4 months in a year. They also collect fuel wood, medicinal herbs, grass, bamboo and timber from the forest for their day-to-day use like building their houses and making agricultural, hunting and fishing implements, cooking, treatment of diseases, and globalization. The impact of such changes can be seen in their changing cultural values, occupational structure and role perception.

Histories of Sautars can also be traced from songs and folklore of the tribe. Historians from different region have come and wrote different things regarding them and large populations believe that is only the truth about Sautars.

Music, Dance, Art and Craft are of great importance in their daily lives. The theme of arts are related to nature, festivals, rituals, agriculture, human emotions and simple conversations. Poush Parav dance, Maghe dance, Sarhul dance, Baha dance, Sarhul dance, Langrai dance, Dong dance, Gulwari dance, Sohrai dance, Dasai dance, Dansa dance, Dhonger dance, Morakaram dance and Singrai dance are performed during different occasions.

In economic domain the structure of deprivation saw the upward revision of the rent settlement. Moneylenders took advantage of the new arrangement of imposing rent on tribal land because the tribals in order to pay rent had to borrow money from the mahajans at an exhorbitant rate of interest. Mahajans made the Sautars mortgage their land in lieu of the loan. Subsequently the defaulters were deprived of their own land.

Their most important festivals are Eroksim,Harihar-sim, Iri-Guldi-sim, Janthar, Sahrai, Magha-sim and Baha, which areassociated with agriculture. Festivals like Karma and Makar Sankranti are also celebrated with gait and ceremony for the prosperity and happiness of their community.

The agrarian structure of the Sautars during pre-colonial period was characterised by the communitarian pattern. After the extension of colonial zule in tribal areas the equalitarian arrangements of tribal social system' saw major changes. It reflected in the economic activities of production, distribution and consumption. The imperial design of the colonial state completed its full circle when the tax on land occupied by the Sautars began to be realised in a systematic way with the help of the zamindars. Thus a group of exploiters i.e., zarnindars, moneylenders and the merchants developed vested interest intribal economic resources. The influences of modern values and institution in the form of spread of education, modern technology and migrants, sociologist have noted changes in the social, economic and cultural life of tribals. More particularly the have been exposed to the processes related to modernisation.

❑

References

- BAG, Dhanipati ,1983, *Sautar Samaj Sameeksha - A Study on Sautar Society*; Samatat Prakashani; Calcutta.
- Bahadur, K.P., 1997, *Caste Tribes and Culture of India: Bengal, Bihar and Orissa, Vol. III*, Delhi, ESS ESS Publications.
- Biswas, P.C., 1956, *Sautars of the Sautar Praganas,* Delhi: Bharatiya Adim Jati Sevak Sangh.
- Bodding P.O., *Studies in Sautar medicine and connected folklore*, 1986, The asiatic Society , 1-Park Street, Kolkatta-700016.
- Bodding, P.O. 1925-29. *Sautar Folk Tales*. Oslo: H. Aschehough & Co.[Reprint: 1997. New Delhi: Gyan Publishing House].
- Bodding, P.O., 1942, *Traditions and Institutions of the Sautars*, Oslo: A.W. Broggers Boktrykkeri.
- Bodding, P.O., 1990, *Sautar Folk Tales, Vol. I, II, III*, New Delhi: Gian Publishing House.
- Bodding, P.O., *Traditions and Institutions of the Sautars*, 2001, New Delhi, Gyan.
- Bodding, Paul Olaf, 1993, *Sautari Dictionary*.

- Bompas, C.H., 1981, *Folklore of the Sautar Parganas*, New Delhi: Ajay Book Service.
- Bompas, Cecil Henry (Tr.) *Folklore of the Sautar Parganas*; 324p., Gloss., App., 22 cm. 2001, Delhi.
- Chakrabortti, Digambar, 1989, *History of the Sautar Hool of 1855* (reprinted Calcutta: 1989).
- CHAUDHURI, A.B., *The Sautar Religion and Rituals*; Ashish Publishing House; New Delhi; 1985
- Chaudhuri, A.B., 1993, *State formation among tribals: A quest for Sautar identity,* (New Delhi).
- Choudhury, Asit Baran, *Saontal Samaj, Daini O Bartaman Sankat - The Society of Saontal*; A Mukherjee and Co. Pvt. Ltd.; Calcutta; 1985.
- Culshaw, Wesley J., 1949, *Tribal Heritage: A Study of the Sautars*, London: Lutterworth.
- DASGUPTA, Somesh, 1999, *Human Encounter: The Sautars in a Spider's Clutch and Other stories*; Rupali Computer; Barasat.
- Datta Kalikinkar, *The Sautar insurrection of 1855-57, second ed. 2001*, Firma KLM Pvt Ltd, 257B,BB Ganguly St, Kolkata-700012.
- GAUSDAL, Johannes 1960, *The Sautar Khuts - Contribution to Animistic Research*; Harvard University Press; Cambridge, Mass.
- Hembram, P.C., *Sari-Sarna: Sautar Religion*, 1988, Publisher Mittal , Delhi Hardbound New 6, India. Hembrom Dr T, The Sautars, 1996, Punthi pustak, 136/4B, Bidhansarani, Kolkata-700004.
- Kisku, D. Barka, 2000. *The Sautars and their Ancestors*. Dumka: Career Press.

References

- Kochuchira, John, *Political History of Sautar Parganas : From 1765 to 1872, 2000*, New Delhi, Inter-India, 2000.
- Mahapatra, Mary D., *Tribal Religion and Rituals: Accounts of Superstition*, Sorcery and Spirits, 2001, Delhi, Dominant.
- Mahapatra, Sitakanta, 1987, *Modernization & Ritual*, Oxford University Press, Incorporated.
- Mathur, Nita (Ed.), *Sautar Worldview*. 2001.
- MCALPIN, M.C., 1981, *Report on the Condit. of the Sonthals in Dist. of Birbhum*, Bankura, Midnapore.
- Mitra P C., *Sautari - A universal heritage*, 1991, Firma KLM Pvt Ltd, 257B, BB Ganguly St, Kolkata-700012.
- Mukherjee, C.L. 1962. *The Sautars*. Calcutta: A. Mukherjee.
- Murmu, Gurucharan. 1998. *Bibliography of Sautari Literature*. Calcutta: Biswajnan N. Balasore.; Firma Mukhopadhyay; Calcutta.
- Narayan, Sachindra, 1986, *Dimensions of Development in Tribal Bihar*, New Delhi, Inter-India Publications.
- Neukom, Lukas, 2001. *Sautari. München: Lincom* (Languages of the World/Materials, 323).
- Neukom, Lukas in press. *Argument Marking in Sautari*. In: Mon-Khmer Studies, XXX. New Delhi: Indira Gandhi National Center for the Arts.
- Orans, M. 1965. *The Sautar: A Tribe in Search of a Great Tradition*. Detroit: Wayne State University Press.
- Phillips, Jeremiah, 1845/1852, *A Sautari Primer*. Calcutta: School Book Society.
- Phillips, Jeremiah. 1852. *An Introduction to the Sautari language*, Calcutta.

- RAY, Ujjwal Kanti ; 1982 *To Be With Sautars*; Government of West Bengal; Calcutta.
- Risley H H, *The tribes and castes of Bengal*, 1981, Firma KLM Pvt Ltd, 257B, BB Ganguly, St, Kolkata-700012.